Not Blacl

C000246475

Not Black and White

Category B
Roy Williams

Seize the Day
Kwame Kwei-Armah

Detaining Justice
Bola Agbaje

Methuen Drama

This collection first published in Great Britain in 2009 by Methuen Drama

1 3 5 7 9 10 8 6 4 2

Methuen Drama
A & C Black Publishers Limited
36 Soho Square
London W1D 3QY
www.methuendrama.com

Category B copyright © Roy Williams 2009
Seize the Day copyright © Kwame Kwei-Armah 2009
Detaining Justice copyright © Bola Agbaje 2009

Introduction copyright © Nicolas Kent 2009

The authors have asserted their rights under the Copyright, Designs
and Patents Act, 1988, to be identified as authors of these works

A CIP catalogue record for this book is available from the British Library

ISBN: 978 1 408 12744 5

Typeset by Country Setting, Kingsdown, Kent
Printed and bound in Great Britain by
CPI Cox & Wyman, Reading, Berkshire

Caution

All rights whatsoever in these plays are strictly reserved and application
for performance etc. should be made before rehearsals begin to:
for *Category B* to Alan Brodie Representation Limited, 6th Floor, Fairgate House,
78 New Oxford Street, London WC1A 1HB; for *Seize the Day* and for *Detaining Justice* to
United Agents, 12–26 Lexicon Street, London W1F 0LE. No performance
may be given unless a licence has been obtained.

All rights reserved. No part of this publication may be reproduced in any form
or by any means – graphic, electronic or mechanical, including photocopying,
recording, taping or information storage and retrieval systems – without
the written permission of A & C Black Publishers Limited.

This book is produced using paper that is made from wood grown in managed,
sustainable forests. It is natural, renewable and recyclable. The logging
and manufacturing processes conform to the environmental regulations
of the country of origin.

Contents

Introduction   vii

The Tricycle   ix

CATEGORY B   1

SEIZE THE DAY   103

DETAINING JUSTICE   185

Introduction

Three years ago the Tricycle launched a four-month season with a black ensemble company premiering three plays chronicling the African-American experience in the twentieth century. The season drew large audiences and was a critical success.

As we approached the end of the first decade of the twenty-first century, and across London black and Asian children outnumber white British children by about six to four, I thought it important and challenging to look at the society in which we live from the perspective of black writers.

The Tricycle already had a strong relationship with Roy Williams and Kwame Kwei-Armah, having premiered plays by both writers – as well as both of them being members of our Bloomberg Playwrights Group – so it seemed natural to approach them first. They were very enthusiastic about the idea, and at our first meeting we agreed the areas of British life each would choose as subjects. We also all felt it was essential to have a woman's voice, and all three of us had been very impressed by Bola Agbaje's first play, *Gone Too Far!*, so I was delegated to approach her with a commission to make up the trilogy.

Late last year the four of us had a meeting to define the subject of each play, and the size, gender and racial composition of the company. As the commissions were delivered in the spring and summer of this year, and each went through various different drafts I started to think of a collective title for the season. 'Not Black and White' seemed to encapsulate the ambition of the season: not just because of the ambiguities and complexities that a culturally diverse twenty-first-century London and the plays represented, but also because these views by black playwrights refreshingly did not reference white Londoners and the white establishment – instead they focused primarily on black relationships, as well as black and Asian relationships.

My hope, and that of the playwrights, is that these plays are for London now, and that they reflect the excitement, the complexities and difficulties that a diverse city and society face as we end the first decade of this new millennium.

Nicolas Kent
5 September 2009

The Tricycle Theatre

The Tricycle Theatre has established a unique reputation for presenting plays that reflect the cultural diversity of its community; in particular plays by Black, Irish, Jewish, Asian and South African writers, as well as for responding to contemporary issues and events with its ground-breaking 'tribunal plays'.

In 1994 the Tricycle produced *Half the Picture* by Richard Norton-Taylor and John McGrath (a dramatisation of the Scott Arms to Iraq Inquiry), which was the first play ever to be performed in the Houses of Parliament. The next, marking the fiftieth anniversary of the 1946 War Crimes Tribunal, was *Nuremberg*, which was followed by *Srebrenica* – the UN Rule 61 Hearings, which later transferred to the National Theatre and the Belfast Festival. In 1999, the Tricycle's reconstruction of the Stephen Lawrence Inquiry, *The Colour of Justice*, transferred to the West End. It completed a national tour which included Belfast and the Royal National Theatre in 1999. In 2003 *Justifying War – Scenes from the Hutton Inquiry* opened at the Tricycle. All five of these plays have been broadcast by the BBC, and have together reached audiences of over twenty-five million people worldwide.

In 2004 the Tricycle produced the critically acclaimed *Guantanamo – 'Honor Bound to Defend Freedom'*, written by Victoria Brittain and Gillian Slovo from spoken evidence, which transferred to the West End and New York (where Archbishop Tutu appeared in the production). In 2006 the Tricycle presented a performance of the play at the Houses of Parliament and on Washington's Capitol Hill. It has since been performed around the world and in the US through the 'Guantanamo Reading Project', which developed community productions of readings of the play. Twenty-five have already been held in cities across America.

Bloody Sunday – Scenes from the Saville Inquiry opened at the Tricycle in 2005 to critical acclaim and was also performed in Belfast and Derry, and was later broadcast by the BBC. It also received an Olivier Award for Outstanding Achievement.

Notable theatre productions staged at the Tricycle have included the British premiere of *The Great White Hope* by Howard Sackler (later re-staged for the Royal Shakespeare Company), *The Amen Corner* by James Baldwin (which later transferred to the Lyric Theatre), the world premiere of *Playboy of the West Indies* by Mustapha Matura, which has subsequently received more than twenty productions all over the world, has been televised for BBC Television and has returned for tenth and twentieth anniversary productions; the original Tricycle production of the Fats Waller musical *Ain't Misbehavin'* transferred to the Lyric Theatre in the West End. The South African musical *Kat and the Kings* transferred from the Tricycle Theatre to the Vaudeville Theatre in the West End and won two 1999 Olivier Awards for Best New Musical and Best Actor – awarded to the entire cast. It later transferred to Broadway.

At the beginning of the new millennium highlights included the premiere of Harold Pinter's *The Dwarfs*; and two world premieres of plays about the political situation in Northern Ireland: *As the Beast Sleeps* by Gary Mitchell and *Ten Rounds* by Carlo Gebler (nominated for the Ewart-Biggs prize). The 2002 production of Arthur Miller's *The Price* returned to the Tricycle in 2003 before a successful run at the Apollo Theatre in the West End, and a national tour in 2004.

In 2005/6 the Tricycle pioneered a black ensemble company in three British premieres of African-American plays chronicling the black experience of the last hundred years: *Walk Hard* by Abram Hill, *Gem of the Ocean* by the late August Wilson and *Fabulation* by Lynn Nottage.

Later the same year (together with Fiery Angel Ltd), the Tricycle presented John Buchan's *Thirty-Nine Steps*, adapted by Patrick Barlow, to sell-out houses. This immediately transferred to the Criterion Theatre in the West End, and opened on Broadway in January 2008.

In November 2006, the Tricycle was proud to win a Special Award at the *Evening Standard* Theatre Awards for 'its pioneering political work'.

In 2008 the Tricycle premiered *Radio Golf* – the last of August Wilson's Decalogue chronicling the African-American experience of the twentieth century. The Tricycle has premiered six of August Wilson's plays in Britain.

In the summer of 2009 the Tricycle launched its eight-hour trilogy about Afghanistan: *The Great Game*, which premiered plays by Richard Bean, David Edgar, David Greig, Amit Gupta, Ron Hutchinson, Stephen Jeffreys, Abi Morgan, Ben Ockrent, J. T. Rogers, Simon Stephens, Colin Teevan, Naomi Wallace and Joy Wilkinson.

Education and community activities are an integral part of the artistic output of the Tricycle. Last year there were more than 40,000 attendances by young people to see films and plays, or to take part in workshops.

The Tricycle's home in the London borough of Brent comprises a theatre, cinema, art gallery, café and bar, and it is open all year round.

Roy Williams

Category B

For Noel Greig.
You are loved. You are missed.

Roy Williams

Roy Williams worked as an actor before turning to writing full-time in 1990. He graduated from Rose Bruford in 1995 with a first class BA Hons degree in Writing and participated in the 1997 Carlton Television screenwriter's course. *The No Boys Cricket Club* (Theatre Royal, Stratford East, 1996) won him nominations for the TAPS Writer of the Year Award 1996 and for New Writer of the Year Award 1996 by the Writers' Guild of Great Britain. He was the first recipient of the Alfred Fagon Award 1997 for *Starstruck* (Tricycle Theatre, London, 1998), which also won the 31st John Whiting Award and the EMMA Award 1999. *Lift Off* (Royal Court Theatre Upstairs, 1999) was the joint winner of the George Devine Award 2000. His other plays include: *Night and Day* (Theatre Venture, 1996); *Josie's Boys* (Red Ladder Theatre Co., 1996); *Souls* (Theatre Centre, 1999); *Local Boy* (Hampstead Theatre, 2000); *The Gift* (Birmingham Rep/Tricycle Theatre, 2000); *Clubland* (Royal Court, 2001), winner of the *Evening Standard* Charles Wintour Award for the Most Promising Playwright; *Fallout* (Royal Court Theatre, 2003) which was made for television by Company Pictures/Channel 4; *Sing Yer Heart Out for the Lads* (National Theatre, 2002, 2004), *Little Sweet Thing* (New Wolsey, Ipswich/Nottingham Playhouse/Birmingham Rep, 2005), *Slow Time* (National Theatre Education Department tour, 2005), *Days of Significance* (Swan Theatre, Stratford-upon-Avon, 2007), *Absolute Beginners* (Lyric Theatre, Hammersmith, 2007), *Joe Guy* (Tiata Fahodzi/Soho Theatre, 2007), *Baby Girl* (National Theatre, 2007), *Out of the Fog* (Almeida Theatre, 2007), *There's Only One Wayne Matthews* (Polka Theatre, 2007), and he contributed to *A Chain Play* (Almeida Theatre, 2007). His screenplays include *Offside*, winner of a BAFTA for Best Schools Drama 2002. His radio plays include *Tell Tale*; *Homeboys*, *Westway*, which was broadcast as part of Radio 4 First Bite Young Writers' Festival, and *To Sir with Love*. He also wrote *Babyfather* for BBC TV.

Category B was first performed as part of the 'Not Black and White' season at the Tricycle Theatre, London, on 8 October 2009. The cast, in order of appearance, was as follows:

Angela	Sharon Duncan-Brewster
David	Kobna Holdbrook-Smith
Rio	Aml Ameen
Andy	Robert Whitelock
Saul	Jimmy Akingbola
Riz	
	Abhin Galeya
Errol	Karl Collins
Chandra	Jaye Griffiths
Reece	John Boyega

Director Paulette Randall
Designer Rosa Maggiora
Lighting Designer James Farncombe
Sound Designer Tom Lishman
Costume Supervisor Sydney Florence
Production Manager Shaz McGee
Casting Suzanne Crowley and Gilly Poole

2009/10 new writing for new audiences supported by BLOOMBERG

Characters

Angela, *black, early forties*
Rio, *black, early twenties*
Andy, *white, early forties*
Errol, *black, late thirties*
Saul, *black, mid-twenties*
David, *black, twenties*
Chandra, *black, thirties*
Reece, *black, early twenties*
Riz, *Asian, twenties*

Setting: present day

Location: C Wing, Thames Gate Prison, London.

NB: the exchange between Riz and Yasmin in Part One, Scene Ten, should be spoken completely in Urdu.

Part One

One

Angela *enters.*

Angela   Category B prisons. Or as my colleagues affectionately call them, the shit of the shit! Everyone who goes to a prison is sent to a Cat B first, everyone. The idea is that you get categorised first, then you are sent to an appropriate prison. Cat As for the lifers. You know – murderers, serial rapists, drug dealers. And I ain't chatting about the local boy who you occasionally buy the line of white off in the pub. I mean the hardcore ones, the ones who own planes and boats, that are bringing that shit in here. Cat C are the ones most people go to. From your ABH, drunk drivers to burglars and some cunt caught watching child porn. Cat Ds, otherwise known as open prisons, are for inmates who pose no threat to the general public. Low risk. You know, like tax fraud, perjury, not paying your council tax. Prisoners have their own fucking keys to their cells in a there. No one fucks around in a Cat D, cos no one wants to go to a Cat B prison, no one wants to come here, prisoners and screws alike. On paper that is the way it is supposed to work, but in practice, cos of overcrowding, I've seen inmates serve their entire time in a Cat B prison. Sometimes being a good screw is learning when not to be a good screw, if you follow me. It is learning when to turn a blind eye to certain 'things'. If a little pop keeps them on top, who am I to argue? As long as they don't take the piss or think they own you, I'm down with that. It is all about keeping the pressure. If we didn't keep the pressure, you'd be hearing about riots in prisons every other week. Let's be clear, I ain't bent. I don't have time for bent screws, not in this uniform, no sir! Prisoners don't play me, I play them. What did you expect? They ain't paying us enough to follow their stupid rules. They are the ones who keep bringing bodies in here, especially the brothers, I mean what is up with that? To coin a phrase from the great Richard Pryor, you go in courts looking for justice, that is all you will find; just us!

Two

David *enters.*

David   Angela Richards?

Angela   That'll be me.

David   Saunders, David.

Angela   Pleased to meet you, Saunders David.

David *chuckles.*

Angela   You have a sense of humour, that's good. I like that.
You're early.

David   Yeah, I thought I'd make a start.

Angela   With what?

David   The job.

Angela   You're keen.

David   Is that good as well?

Angela   Your shift does not start for another half hour.
I was hoping you and I could sit down somewhere, have a
coffee, go over a couple of things.

David   If it's alright, I would like to hit the ground running.
If you don't mind?

Angela   No, I don't mind.

David   I'm like that. Besides, I bet you're eager to go.

Angela   Still got another few weeks.

David   Of course, but you know . . .

Angela   Know what?

David   It will just make this transition time easy for both of
us. Only thinking of you.

Angela   How kind.

David Shall we?

Angela Just answer me this. What you doing here?

David What?

Angela Here, doing, what, you?

David I'm not following you.

Angela Why did you ask to come here? Why request it? Why go out of your way? I've never heard or known any screw who wants to bring their arse here.

David Well, what made you want to come here?

Angela Oh, answering a question with a question.

David Is that good?

Angela No, it's not. I hate that. I really hate that. And I'd appreciate it if you didn't presume to know me, yeah?

David Fair enough.

Angela It ain't about fair, it's about what it is.

David I thought I could do some good. Does that answer your question?

Angela Some good?

David Is there a problem?

Angela Here?

David Why don't we start again?

Angela Why not? Officer Simmonds . . .

David Saunders.

Angela . . . Saunders, welcome to the shit. For the next few weeks you are with me, and only me. You look, you listen and speak only when you have something to say. When we're done here, I will take you for a walk around the landings.

David I have something to say.

Angela Yes?

David   I have been an officer for two years now. In that time I worked at . . .

Angela   Rainesworth Prison, Cat D.

David   That's right.

Angela   Rainesworth Prison is the bloody Hilton compared to here. Which is where you are, love. The shit. Shall we?

David   You're the boss.

Three

Andy *enters, followed by a prisoner,* **Rio**.

Angela   Rio Anderson?

Rio   I'm Rio, but . . .

Angela   I'm Officer Richards. This ugly one here is Officer Maggs, this one is . . . sorry . . . ?

David   Saunders.

Angela   Right, he's Sanders. We're going to look after you, yes?

Rio   Yeah.

Angela   Could you lift your head up, please?

Rio *lifts his head.*

Angela   That's better. (*Aside.*) What do you think?

Andy   He'll be crying for his mum by midnight.

Angela   Looks like a hard one to me.

Andy   Should have gone to Specsavers. He don't look like he's starting shaving.

Rio   I ain't crying for nobody.

Andy   Excuse me, what was that?

Rio   I said I ain't crying for nobody.

Andy   Hey!

Rio   You understand?

Andy   Hold your tongue, do it now. I think he wants to break the world record, this one.

David   For what?

Andy   Being dropped. Fancy that, do yer, Anderson?

Rio   It's Baptiste.

Angela   I've got you written down as Anderson.

Rio   It's Baptiste, I know my name.

Andy   Be nice.

Angela   I swear to Christ, if they've sent us the wrong body . . .

Andy   Better than sending out the wrong body, I suppose.

Angela   Here we go. How long are you going to keep mouthing on about that?

Andy   Until it stops being funny.

Angela   Suck my dick.

Andy   Careful, Ange, you are making our new boy blush.

Angela   Don't let him teach you any bad habits, Sanders.

David   Saunders.

Andy   You and Errol have been going at it lately, what's that about?

Angela   Yer asking me?

Andy   Would you like me to have a little *career chat* with him?

Angela   Thank you, Andrew, but that will not be necessary. (*To* **Rio**.) Right, so, who the hell are you then, and what are you doing in my nick?

Rio   Anderson is my middle name, they must have left it out by mistake.

Andy   Or couldn't be arsed.

Angela   Why would your mother give you a middle name like Anderson?

Rio   It's her mum's maiden name, my gran.

Angela   Something wrong with your mother's maiden name?

Rio   I'm using it, Baptiste.

Angela   So what did your dad do to deserve you not having his name?

Rio   He weren't around.

Angela   Yeah, that'll do it. Rio Anderson Baptiste, welcome to Thames Gate Hilton. We do hope you enjoy your stay.

Andy   Are you hanging round for any particular reason, Ange?

Angela   Seen one pair and you've seen them all. I'll leave you arse bandits to it then. See you on the other side, Rio. You as well, David, come find me, yeah.

Angela *leaves.*

Andy   OK, empty your pockets and put them over here.

Rio *does as he is told.*

Andy   Right, now strip.

Rio   'Scuse?

Andy   Clothes, off, and you don't say 'scuse. You say Sir, Guv, or Mister Maggs. Your choice. Now off.

Rio   What?

David (*raises his voice*)   Clothes!

Andy (*whispers*)   Off. Now.

Rio *takes off his clothes.*

Andy   Oi, Simpson?

David   Saunders.

Andy   I don't think there is anything wrong with his hearing. No need to bellow, mate.

David   Right, sorry.

Andy   Well, don't be shy.

David *picks ups* **Rio**'s *clothes and places them in a bag.*

Andy   Christ knows where we are going to put you, jammed solid as it is. Please tell me they gave you something to eat.

Rio   I'm good.

Andy   Is that an answer, yes or no?

Rio   Yes.

Andy   Yes, that is an answer, or yes or no, did you eat?

Rio   I ate.

Andy   Good, just as well cos the kitchen is closed. Your watch.

Rio   Can't I keep it?

Andy   No, you can't.

Rio *hands over the watch. In return,* **David** *hands* **Rio** *his prison clothes.*

Andy   Those are your clothes.

Rio *begins to get changed.*

Andy   No, hold up. Tad eager, aren't we? You have to shower first. Might not even fit – if they don't, let us know as soon as possible, alright?

Rio   Yes.

Andy   Yes, what?

Rio   Sir.

Andy   Good lad. (*To* **David**.) So, what am I forgetting?

David   Number?

Andy   You're sharp

David   Thank you.

Andy   We like you. Well?

David (*reads from form*)   FB4832. Can you repeat that, please?

Rio   FB4832.

Andy   That's your number. You will need to remember that. Do you like jobs?

Rio   Yes, sir.

Andy   We'll find you a job. We're going to give you some forms to read, about some of the lessons we do here. If you see any you like, you can get back to us.

Rio   Safe, Sir!

Andy   Much better. Sanders? With feeling.

David   Do not steal from your fellow prisoners. Do not smoke on your bed. Do not seal your outgoing mail. Do not play-fight with your cellmate. Do not lend or borrow. Do not make holes in the walls. Do not graffiti on the furniture. Do not damage any prison property. Good?

Andy   Sanders, I am sexually aroused.

David   It's Saunders.

Andy (*to* **Rio**)   Get used to it, son, you live here now. Let's go.

Four

Saul *struts around the landing like he runs the entire prison. As far as a lot of the inmates are concerned, he does. He sits with* **Riz**.

Riz I love old films. Love them! I used to watch them with my dad, he had his own private stash. VHS, old shit. Each tape was set to play his favourite scenes, so he didn't have to waste time fast-forwarding. You ever seen *Stripes*, Saul? That was one of my favourites. It's the one with that bloke from *Ghostbusters*. There's this scene yeah, where the main army guy, Major or summin, total perv, is in his office, looking into the women soldiers' showers with his telescope . . . So he sees them all naked, yeah? And he's telling one, with the finest pair ever, to wash off the soap, and she does with her hands, like she can hear him, boy! *'Yeah baby, wash off the soap.'* I loved that film. Class. The other oldie I like is *The Stud* with Joan Collins? She might be old now, but that gal had it going on for her when she was young, man. That scene when she's in the baths, she's totally naked, man, grinding some brer on the swing, no less! Joke is, his wife is down in the pool, grinding some other guy, who is supposed to be grinding Joan Collins then the man next! But he couldn't get it up, so they dashed him. Now why can't I be invited to parties like that? Saul?

Saul Sorry, Riz, I didn't realise you stopped talking.

Riz Dass cool. (*Quotes.*) 'What is thy bidding, my master?'

Saul (*sighs*)   *Star Wars*?

Riz *Empire Strikes Back* actually. But if you said *Return of the Jedi*, you would have been right as well. Cos he says it again in *Return of the Jedi* . . .

Saul I don't give a fuck, Riz. And you got company.

Errol *enters, looking for* **Riz**.

Errol Is that fucking Riz out here?

Riz You want summin, brother?

Errol What the fuck you think is going on here, Riz?

Riz Who you talking to like that?

Errol You, you rag-head fuck!

Riz I think you better mind who you chatting to here.

Errol (*grabs his crotch*)   Chat this!

Riz   Step!

Errol   You think I care?

Riz   No, but I think you had better start caring, right now.

Errol   You must think this shit yer going on with is the will of Allah or summin. Well, Allah ain't too smart, neither are you. You can tell Allah that he can kiss my black beautiful Church of England arse, I'm tired of you Muslims acting like you are all that.

Riz (*quotes*)   'I find your lack of faith disturbing.'

Errol   Don't even start that.

Riz (*quotes*)   'Do you think you have been treated unfairly?'

Errol   My money!

Riz   My shit?

Errol   Flushed it away, you call that shit?

Riz   I don't see anyone complaining. Now move yer whining arse away from me before I melt yer.

Errol   I ain't playing, Riz.

Riz   You think I am?

Errol   That shit was bogus, you know it. Now I want some proper pills and I want them now.

Riz   You had them, you flushed them. (*Quotes.*) 'I have you now.'

Errol   How high was I fucking supposed to get with that?

Riz   Almost as high as you are now. Like some fucking vent, like yer about to blow. Look around, bitch, anyone who got eyes will say the same. Now get the fuck outta my face before you make a scene. Carrying on like I've got shit coming out of every hole. Even if I did, you think I'm stupid enough to be giving it out for free? Go back to yer cell and wake up again.

Errol   I want my pills. That I paid for.

Riz   I want me a woman. Angelina Jolie, you have her stuffed down yer pants?

Errol   Riz?

Riz   Fuck off.

Errol   Yeah, I'll fuck off.

Riz   Thank you.

Errol   I'll fuck right off to the screws, have a whisper in their ear and shit, spin yer cell. Loss of privileges for a month, nigger. Think I won't?

Riz   Think I care? I oughta rip yer tongue out, bout you saying that shit to me.

Errol   Do what yu gotta, Osama!

Riz   I will start on yer balls and work my up if you call me that again.

Errol   Add this to your thinking. Every junkie inmate in here getting in line to go medieval on yer arse, ca you bin fleecing them. I'm heading out.

Riz   Errol, Errol, my man. Errol? Errol, will you just stand still and wait a fucking minute, please? Just stand the fuck still yeah, can you do that for me?

Errol   Wass it worth?

Riz   Just wait.

Riz finds some pills on his person. At this point, **Angela,** *who has been watching this from the first-floor landing, chooses to look the other way. She motions* **David** *to do the same.*

Riz hands **Errol** *some pills.*

Riz   You get in my face like that again and I will peel you like an onion. (*Quotes.*) 'You will truly know the full power of the dark side.'

Errol It's . . . (*Quotes.*) 'If you only knew the power of the dark side.' Just after he chop Luke's hand and before he tell him he's his dad. If you are going to quote, do it right, yer dumb shit.

Errol *leaves.* **Riz** *rejoins* **Saul***.*

Riz Mother fucker, mother fuck – did you hear that, Saul? Did you hear that?

Saul Calm the fuck down.

Riz Correcting me, there ain't nuttin I don't know about *Star Wars*, nuttin! (*Calls.*) For yer information bitch, hey, Errol! I didn't misquote, The Emperor said that line to Luke in *Return of the Jedi*, so step, step Errol!

Saul Are you done?

Riz What?

Saul *blows in* **Riz***'s ear.*

Riz Saul, what the fuck, man! You want sex, buy me dinner first.

Saul Looks like you just got fucked though, truly. I just wanted to know how easy it is for you to fall and bend over.

Riz Well it ain't, trust.

Saul So why you cave like that?

Riz I don't need the grief.

Saul Yeah, but Angela had our back, didn't you see her?

Riz Obviously not.

Saul Dumb arse.

Riz What is this, get on fucking Riz's day?

Saul Calm yerself – for what it's worth, I think you did the right thing.

Riz Thank you.

Saul   But I catch you selling bogus shit again, ever, and it's you that's flying off the landing, *capice*?

Riz   I'm just making the good stuff last longer. Your instructions.

Saul   Errol's no fool. Don't fuck with him.

Riz   He ain't all that.

Saul   Brer accused him of cheating at Trivial Pursuit one time. Errol fed the cards to him, one by one.

Riz (*quotes*)   Impressive. Most impressive.

Saul   You wanna die? So, we on top of everything? Accounts in order?

Riz   Yeah, blud, we're safe.

Saul   Couldn't help but wonder we seem to be coming up a little short lately.

Riz   Yeah, well, you know how it is out there, Saul. It's crunch time. Tightening of belts and shit. It was only a matter of time before the ripple reach us.

Saul   Must be.

Angela *and* **David** *come down on to the floor.*

David   Is this how it is played around here? Don't ask, don't tell? (*Waits for reply.*) You are going to love this. First nick I was in, yeah, a group of prisoners were acting in some play with a theatre company outside. They were performing to an invited audience from outside. One of the prisoners had to wear a suit and tie for his character. He wore it so well, when the show finished a couple of dozy screws, not me I might add, let him out with the rest of the audience, and I mean let out, by the alarm was raised, he was helping himself to a nice pub lunch. Sunday roast, he claimed. Anyway we got him back, but the shit the Governor was raising was . . .

Angela   Yeah, triffic, do me a favour, stop talking, eh, Smithers?

David (*mutters*)   It's Saunders.

Angela *approaches* **Saul** *and* **Riz**. *They see her coming and try to leave.*

Angela   Sit yer arses down.

Saul   Yes, Miss!

Riz   You alright?

Angela   Do I look?

She throws down one training shoe.

Angela   Well?

Saul   Nuttin to say, Miss

Angela   Don't give me that.

Riz   What, man?

Angela   You know bloody what?

Riz   Daze, man.

Angela   No one moves until they tell me.

Saul   Miss, what is it that you want?

Angela   The truth. Now I know that is a concept lost on you boys. But trust me on this, now is not the time to be fucking with me. Do you understand? (*Hears them mutter.*) I can't hear you.

Saul   OK, man.

Angela   Right. So, one last chance, alright?

Saul   Whatever.

Angela   And I want a straight answer out of you lot, is that understood?

Riz   Cool.

Angela   I'm serious.

Riz   Bring it on.

Angela   Right. Do you think he'll go for this?

The boys roar with laughter.

Oh, what's your fucking problem now, eh?

Saul   You are not supposed to swear.

Angela   Never mind that, what is your problems with these ones? What's wrong with them?

Riz   Other than the fact I wouldn't be seen dead in them, nothing at all, Ange.

Angela   They look alright to me, and don't call me Ange.

Riz   How old is your boy?

Angela   Fifteen.

Riz   Well, if he has any sense . . .

Angela   He has.

Saul   Must take after his mum den.

Angela   Leave it!

Riz   Point I'm trying to make, Miss, chances are, if he has any sense, yer boy, like most boys, are gonna be reaching for the latest gear, not this shit.

Angela   Hey, hey, this shit cost me forty quid.

Riz   The prosecution rests.

Angela   So, pray tell, what is the latest gear?

Riz   Well. It depends.

Angela   On what?

Riz   How much more dough you putting on the table.

Angela   I suppose I can push it to fifty.

Riz   Fifty?

Angela   Alright, sixty!

Riz Come on, Miss, this is your son we're talking about here, dig deep.

Angela Alright, how much are we talking?

Riz *and* **Saul** *nod in agreement.*

Riz Ninety?

Angela Ninety!

Riz At least.

Angela Christ!

Riz You'll thank us for that?

Angela What fucking trainers are worth ninety quid?

Riz Air Forces Obama.

Angela What?

Riz Trust me, they're the lick. That's all you need to know When you put them on, man, it's like yer walking on air. I got a pair waiting for me for when I get out. That's if my brother ain't fleeced dem yet. They come in silver, black, varsity red. I got varsity red. Telling you, Miss, you buy them for him – (*points to the other trainers*) throw this in the river, yer son will be bigging you up, guaranteed.

Angela I believe that when I see it.

Saul Feeling the stress, Miss?

Angela That's none of yer business.

Riz Go spoil yer kid, man.

Angela And who are you to give me advice? (*Chuckles.*) Jesus.

Riz All kids love to get spoilt, no matter how old.

Angela Were you spoilt?

Riz Believe.

Angela A lot?

Riz   Nuff times.

Angela   So, what are you doing here then?

Riz   Stopped getting it.

Angela   Don't gimme that. Yer a fucking little thief, that's the only reason yer here.

Riz   Are you going to throw those in the river?

Angela   No, I am not going to throw those into the river. I'm going to wrap them up and give them to my son for his birthday, and he is going to learn what I had to learn when I was his age: take what is given to you, and be grateful. Thank you for your advice.

Riz   Looks like we ain't the only one who stopped getting it.

Angela   Don't. I'm not your mum.

Riz   You don't know my mum.

Tell yer boy we said happy birthday.

Angela   They really make you feel yer walking on air?

Riz   Trust me, Ange.

Angela   Stop calling me Ange.

Riz   Gospel, Miss.

Angela   And he'll be bigging me up, you say?

Riz   From the rooftops. (*Laughs.*)

Angela   What?

Riz   You know yer buying them.

Angela   I'll think about it.

Riz   Yer there already, dread!

The boys finally notice **David**.

Saul   Does he talk?

Angela   Oh, he talks.

David (*aside*)   What's the Asian in for?

Angela   You don't ask what they are in for. Didn't your last nick tell you that?

David   But we ain't in my last nick.

Angela   Read the file. Don't ask them direct. Better yet, don't ask at all. It clouds your judgement. Understand?

David   Perfectly. (*To* **Riz**.) What you in for?

Riz   Doing three years.

David   I mean what did you do?

Riz   I get catch.

The guys chuckle.

David   He thinks he's funny.

Angela   A word.

Saul   Yes, Miss, spank him!

Angela *takes* **David** *aside.*

David   I know what you're going to say.

Angela   No need for me to say it then.

David   I didn't mean anything by it.

Angela   I would hate to be around when you do mean it. Listen up, Dave,

David   David.

Angela   Don't bring that training-school shit here. This lot will eat you alive.

David   It was just a question, I am not stupid.

Angela   Have you ever dropped anybody, David?

David   Not yet.

Angela   Not yet? Little bit eager, aren't we?

David   I'm just prepared.

Angela   What are you doing here?

David   Because I asked.

Angela   Yes, you asked to be assigned here, but why?

David   I told you. I thought I could do some good. I want to learn. But don't treat me like a novice.

Angela   Well, learn this, I run a tight ship on this wing. This lot here, they know the line, as long as they do not cross it, do not take the piss, everyone is happy. Be tough, but be fair. Don't ever lie to them, they know bullshit when they smell it. If they play the game, give them a treat, if they fuck up, give them a treat as long as they are sorry. If they are not, tell them to fuck off. If they touch you, threaten you, get in your face in any way, drop them. Easy. Do you think you can play along?

David   Like I said, I am here to learn.

Andy *approaches.*

Andy   Don't be sucking her cock just yet, David. If she gives you trouble, just ask her why some of the inmates call her Horse.

Angela   Excuse me, Andrew, but I am in the middle of a tour here.

Andy   Yeah, and I am not merely the senior officer around here but the Queen's pet poodle.

Angela   Fine, tell him then.

David   Tell me what?

Angela   Your audience awaits you, Sir.

Andy   It was four years ago. Angela must have been, what, three, four months on the job.

Angela   It was six.

Andy   No, shorter than that.

Angela   Six, Andy.

Andy   Mouth closed, you, I am telling the story.

Angela   Well, tell it right then.

Andy   Alright, she was six months in. We had to deal with this sort who we believed had drugs smuggled in to him after a visit. So, we take him to the search room, we give him the usual spiel, 'We have brought you into this room to do a strip search, as we have a strong suspicion that you may have something that you shouldn't have, blah, blah, blah.' This cunt, a lifer, goes mental, we had to drop him to the floor to restrain him. Madam here is outside on guard. We drag the fella out, all bent up, he catches sight of her, now he hasn't seen a woman for months now. So one glance at her, and she catches the full load. 'You fucking bitch cunt, gonna get my cock and shove it right up yer till you can't breathe you shit. Gonna cut yer head off and shove it up yer arse. You fucking ugly big-teethed black bitch whore. You look like a horse, love.' Well, that was it, solitary for that charmer. And I admit, we had to go into his cell to have a 'career chat' with him. Plus Basic Regime for as long as we feel. He was a mental case. Never left his cell. Doped up to the eyeballs, only way to keep him calm. But Madam here wasn't going to let that lie.

Angela   No sir!

Andy   Believe! She personally arranged for herself to be put on the night shift, for a whole month. Pissed her hubby off no end. Every night, as she walked past charmer's cell, she would lift up the flap, show off the full range of her pearly whites, and go – (*mimics a horse*) 'Neigh, neigh'. Tormented the bastard with that for a whole month she did. When the Governor found out, he was not happy. Never seen an officer put on report so fast.

Angela   I wasn't having him knocking my teeth.

Andy   Bloody lucky you weren't suspended.

Angela   How's the new boy?

Andy   Moody. Has a bit of a mouth on him.

Angela   I am sure you will knock that out of him.

Andy   If he isn't very careful.

Angela   Tell David here how many inmates you've dropped.

Andy   I almost felt sorry for him till I read what he was in for. Piece of shit.

Angela   Better get someone to watch over him.

Andy   You can always ask your boyfriend Saul, couldn't you, Angela?

Angela   Very funny, Andrew. Very funny. Let's see how funny you are eating a doner kebab with no teeth.

Errol *approaches*

Angela   Yes, Errol?

Errol   I wanna switch cells, Miss.

Andy and **Angela** *roar with laughter.*

Errol   What? No joke, right!

Andy   Fucking useless they are, David. Useless and worthless, most if not all. But some, like Errol here, are always good for a laugh. Anything else you would like, Errol – Halle Berry, for example?

Errol   No, just a switch to another cell.

Angela   Come on Errol, not now.

Errol   Did you hear me?

Angela   Every word.

Andy   Run along, Errol.

Errol   You fucking deaf cunt!

Andy   Oi!

Angela   Manners, Errol.

Andy   Take a walk, right fucking now.

Errol   Gimme what I want?

Angela   Errol, we talked about this, remember?

Errol   Shut up and gimme.

Andy   I will give you something.

Errol   Gimme!

Andy   Read my lips. No fucking cell moves!

Angela   This ain't you, Errol, what's going on?

Andy   Are you still here?

Errol *flips. He grabs* **Angela** *and holds her by the throat with a dining knife.*

Errol   Back off! Back off!

Andy   Alright, we're backing off. So, what's this all about, Errol? I mean, I know Spurs lost four–nil this week, but this is taking it a little bit too far, don't you think?

Errol   I want my cell move.

Andy   Alright, well, let's talk about that, but you know the game, Errol, better than most.

Errol   You think I'm stupid.

Andy   I would never think that.

Errol   Bollocks!

Andy   I don't lie to anybody, Errol, you know that. You know me. I don't think yer stupid. Fucking mental, yes, but not stupid. Put the knife down and let's talk, like a couple of grown-ups.

He sees the inmates gathering to watch.

You lot, fuck off!

Riz   Don't think so. Better than tele, blud.

Errol   Not gonna let you do it, not gonna let any of you do this to me.

Andy   I give up, he's not making sense.

Angela   Just like a man, Andrew, leave it to the woman.

Andy   I'm calling it in, David?

Angela   Just hold up. Errol, listen to me. Yer not going to hurt me, cos yer a good man, a stand up. You looked after me when I first come here, showed me what's what, remember? Come on, darling, look at me. Look at my face, you seriously wanna hurt me, you woulda done it by now, you know that. Why don't you just lower the knife for me, eh? Please?

Errol *lowers the knife.* **Angela** *breaks free.* **Andy** *embraces her.*

Andy   I thought I had lost you, girl

Angela   Time and place, Andrew. Will somebody drop him?

David (*eager*)   I'll do him.

David *holds* **Errol** *down. He screams.*

Angela (*protesting*)   Hey!

Five

Errol *sees* **Chandra** *in the visiting room. He crosses over to her.* **Chandra** *sees his face.*

Chandra   What happened to you?

Errol   One of the screws decided to give me a piece of his mind.

Chandra   What did you do?

Errol   Me? Why is it always me?

Chandra   Cos I know you.

Errol   Might have changed.

Chandra   In a parallel universe.

Errol   Well, you certainly haven't changed. You and your mouth. I held a knife to a screw's neck. I think they are a little pissed off about that.

Chandra   Look at you, Errol, like the bad boy thing still works.

Errol   You done?

Chandra   How old are you?

Errol   Did I come all the way down here for this?

Chandra   No, you didn't.

Errol   Well, say what you have to say then?

Chandra   Yes, cos you've got so much to do today, haven't you?

Errol *rises from his chair.*

Chandra   Oh sit down, man.

Errol   Long way by train was it?

Chandra   It is a long way, but I drove.

Errol   You drive?

Chandra   I got over my fear of driving years back.

Errol   I'm impressed. The thought of seeing you behind the wheel, though. Sorry you had to come out all this way.

Chandra   Not a problem. I just used my sat-nav.

Errol   Would you believe me if I told you I've never seen one of those? How's yer mum?

Chandra   Fine.

Errol   Still hates me?

Chandra   Beyond belief.

Errol   You really favour her, man. As you get older.

Chandra   Thank you.

Errol   I mean, you don't have her eyes, but that look, the way you tilt your head.

Chandra   You're unbelievable.

Errol   No, no, listen. You still got it going on, girl. You look beautiful.

Chandra   How long we have?

Errol   An hour. But you can go whenever you want.

Chandra   That is not what I want, it's not what I meant. I'm . . . I just don't know what to say to you.

Errol   Maybe you are trying too hard.

Chandra   Maybe.

Errol   I still remember how you used to smile.

Chandra   Please, don't.

Errol   Well, tell me about yourself. What are you doing? Gimme a catch-up.

Chandra   Still in Tesco's. Shelf-stacking.

Errol   Oh, good for you.

Chandra   Shut up. I work in head office. Admin.

Errol   Nice.

Chandra   Only part-time. Doing Open University.

Errol   Shut up.

Chandra   You wanna die?

Errol   Bring it.

Chandra   I'll fling it.

Errol *and* **Chandra**   Flaunt it.

They chuckle.

Errol   So, you go have letters after your name and that?

Chandra   If I see it through.

Errol   You'll see it through. You see everything through.

Chandra   Except you. I didn't see you through.

Errol   I'm the one who left, Chandra. Don't beat yourself up.

Chandra   I'm not.

Pause.

Errol   Now we're back to silence.

Chandra   I'm sorry. This is more difficult than I thought. I mean it's you, really you. Ca I ask you something?

Errol   Shoot.

Chandra   Did you do it?

Errol   What difference would it make?

Chandra   Because that is not the Errol I remember. That's not the Errol who used to write me beautiful letters. I couldn't believe what they said about you, that you could . . . I never saw that side when we were together. Selfish? Yes. Immature? Most definitely, but I never had you down as . . .

Errol   What?

Chandra   Did you do it?

Errol   I'm here, aren't I? They banged me up for it.

Chandra   Did you do it, Errol?

Errol   Did I kill him? Yes, I did.

Chandra   You murdered him?

Errol   I didn't murder anybody. But I did kill him. Look, if you're uncomfortable, you should go.

Chandra   Do you want me to?

Errol   Yeah, that's what I want, I got plenty of people hating me already, Chandra, and that's fine, that's fine, no more than I deserve. I don't need it from you too. I ain't seen yer arse from time.

Chandra   Eighteen years.

Errol   So I already know how much you hate me.

Chandra   You think I hate you?

Errol   Then why ask all of these questions then? Looking at me like that. I'm tired, girl, I've done my time.

Chandra   Done?

Errol   I'm up for parole in a few weeks.

Chandra   Congratulations.

Errol   Thanks.

Chandra   Do you think you'll get it?

Errol   I'll get it.

Chandra   Even though you're putting blades to people's necks?

Errol   Trust me.

Chandra   I was hoping you would do something for me?

Errol   In here?

Chandra   Yes.

Errol   Alright.

Chandra   You don't even know what the favour is.

Errol   There's nuttin I wouldn't do for you.

Chandra   Except stay with me.

Errol   Yeah, except that. So, what?

Chandra   You remember my little boy, Rio?

Errol   Yer eldest? Yeah, I remember him. He must be a big man by now. What's he doing? Footie? Uni?

Chandra   He's here.

Errol   Say that again?

Chandra   I said he's in here, Errol, with you.

Errol   Shut up.

Chandra   I wish.

Errol   No.

Chandra   Oh yes.

Errol   For real?

Chandra   I just said.

Errol   He get bang up, in here?

Chandra   Yes, Errol, he get bang up.

Errol   No, man!

Chandra   Oh, Errol!

Errol   No! Little Rio, with the cute little smile.

Chandra   Please?

Errol   But when he used to laugh, it was like music.

Chandra   Look, don't make this harder than it is for me. He done wrong. He is here, get over it.

Errol   Alright, I'm sorry, can't be easy for you, having one of yer own out here, but Rio!

Chandra   Errol!

Errol   Alright, I'll shut up. Just tell me, how the fuck you let this . . .

Chandra   Don't talk to me like that, don't even look at me like that. I got three youths, three different dads, I can't keep my eye 24/7. You think I born him for this? I wanted this? To end up here?

Errol   Alright.

Chandra   I would like you . . . I would appreciate if you keep an eye on him for me? He's on remand, watch over him.

Errol   It's a big place you know, Chandra.

Chandra   If you . . . you know, pass him. Look, you must know how hard it was for me to ask you this. Are you going to do this for me or not?

Errol   Maybe.

Chandra   Maybe you will or won't?

Errol   What the fuck did he do?

Chandra   That's not important.

Errol   Chandra?

Chandra   I said that is not important. I'm not telling you. And don't you dare ask neither, don't you dare, Errol. All I want is for you to look after him, do you think you can manage that? I saw what one of these places did to my brother. Rio is not ending up like that, I don't care what he's done, I won't let it. He is still my baby, I still have to look after him, yeah?

Errol   Look, I can't hold his hand or nuttin. Not in here.

Chandra   Just do what you can for him, please?

Errol   I just said I would – you deaf?

Chandra   Is who you chatting breeze to, wid yer rubber lips?

Errol   Is who you stepping to, wid yer chicken legs?

They chuckle.

I still can't believe it Chandra, Rio! Two years old, and he was already breaking hearts.

Chandra   He still has it, when he tries.

Errol   When he tries. 'When you try, Errol.' Remember?

Chandra   I remember.

Errol   You used to run that same shit pass me.

Chandra   For all the good it did.

Errol   Don't say that.

Chandra   I'll say what I like. My ex-man and my boy in the same place. Couldn't make that up. Is it me, was it me, Errol?

Errol   It was never you.

Chandra   So why does every man I love leave me?

Errol   Listen, Chandra, hear me. It was never you. Please stop, stop it, don't look at me like that. Look, you want go, go.

Chandra   Rio?

Errol   I'll see what I can do.

Chandra   Take care of my baby, Errol.

Six

Andy *is with* **Angela** *and* **David**.

Andy   You should have gone straight home.

Angela   And break the rule?

Andy   Fuck the rule.

Angela   When things like this happen, we are all there for each other, no matter. Your words, dread.

Andy   Think of them as merely guidelines. I don't get this, you've had inmates come at you before.

Angela   Yeah, but Errol? You ever known him to be all violent? What has gotten into him?

David   The feeling of this. (*Waves his baton.*)

Angela   David, do you want to step outside?

David   I'm sorry?

Angela   Just for a minute?

David *leaves reluctantly.*

Angela   I saw Errol before, rowing with Saul's boy Riz. He claims he was selling shit.

Andy   So go take it up with Saul.

Angela   Intend to.

Andy   You know I . . . I thought I was going to lose you today.

Angela   Stop it. I'll drop yer

She tries coming on to him.

Andy   Ange?

Angela   Yes?

Andy   What are you doing?

Angela   Well, I think I am trying to sex you here.

Andy   Well, don't.

Angela   Don't? Don't? I tell you, Andrew, sometimes I have to wonder if you bat for the other team.

Andy   You promised you wouldn't do this no more. Stop it, Ange, I ain't got time. See the amount of forms we have to fill in now, bloody untold forms. Make a report, draft a statement.

Angela   Yes, about that –

Andy   That fucking Errol ain't going anywhere now.

Angela   Don't write it. Don't write the report.

Andy   Ange, I have to.

Angela   You don't have to. Just make this one go away, yeah?

Andy   What?

Angela   No one needs to know what Errol did.

Andy   Are you out of your fucking tree?

Angela   Just listen.

Andy   No, I won't listen. He had you by the throat, Ange.

Angela   Yes, Andy, I was there.

Andy   With a knife.

Angela   Why would he do that?

Andy   Why the fuck would you want to cover it up?

Angela   Ain't like the first time we covered shit up on this wing?

Andy   Answer the question.

Angela   How many times have I covered for you, whenever you get the shakes to run to the betting shop?

Andy   This ain't about me.

Angela   Blown your wages again? I bet you have.

Andy   Ange?

Angela   Errol is a snitch. He's one of mine.

Andy   Bollocks.

Angela   No lie.

Andy   Bullshit. Since when?

Angela   A while.

Andy   Bullshit. You never said.

Angela   Yeah, well, he's sensitive. He's not one of my regulars, he just likes to give me the head-ups every now and then. He came to me with fucking good intel.

Andy   Bullshit.

Angela   Andy?

Andy   Bullshit. How good? How good intel?

Angela   He claims Saul is getting a phone smuggled in.

Andy   Oh, bullshit. Bullshit.

Angela   Sounded good to me.

Andy   Mobile phones? On our wing? I don't think so. This is bullshit.

Angela   You need a thesaurus, dread.

Andy   Look, a couple of grams up the batty hole is one thing. But if anyone of them got away with having phones rammed up their arse, they deserve to keep them. Give them a medal. Mobile phones, bullshit . . . I can't believe you fell for this.

Angela   I been doing this job as long as you, Andrew. I know the difference between a con feeding me rubbish and one who's speaking gospel. Trust me, Errol is the latter.

Andy   Why would he tell you this, he's up for parole? Least, he was.

Angela   He says it's a screw bringing it in.

Andy   Come again?

Angela   Yeah, that's the face I pulled. Like you always say, Andy, turning the occasional blind eye to a few grams is one thing, but a mobile phone is taking the piss.

Andy   Alright then, who?

Angela   He wouldn't tell me.

Andy   Oh, Ange!

Angela   Cool yer jets for a second, please.

Andy   The brer is playing you. One last practical joke before he wanders off into the sunset

Angela   Did you not hear me say I believe him? He won't tell me jack until I write him a letter of recommendation to the parole board, model prisoner, all that shit. That little stunt today was his way of telling me to hurry the fuck up!

Andy   You telling me that was staged? You and him?

Angela   It's a code, letting me know Saul has definitely got the phone.

Andy   So that's why you two have been going at it lately?

Angela   Duh! Don't write that report, Andy. You hate bent screws as much as I do.

Andy   Scum of the earth.

Angela   So let's have him.

Andy   What about laughing boy out there?

Angela   I can handle him. I'll just school him with the what-happens-in-the-wing-stays-in-the-wing speech. He'll lap it up. Andy? Andrew?

Andy   I don' believe this.

Angela   You know it makes sense.

Andy   This had be better be good, Ange.

Angela   Thank you. Now, where were we?

She starts kissing him.

Andy   Stop it, Ange.

Angela   Lock the door.

Andy   You don't have to do this.

Angela   I know.

Andy   I thought we weren't doing this again – stop it.

Angela   Fuck me, silly man, you can do that, can't you?

Andy   I can do that. I want to do that.

Angela   So, come.

Andy   Talk to me.

Angela   Isn't that what I am doing? Can you not see my lips moving?

Andy   You tell me?

Angela   Forget it then. You had your chance.

Andy   He had you by the neck and you're freaking out.

Angela   We've just been over this.

Andy   You want to forget what happened, it's like I keep telling you, think of something else. Something good. Let that be your const –

Angela   – Let that be your constant, yes, I got it!

Andy   How is Joel?

Angela   Joel?

Andy   Your husband, Ange.

Angela   Since when you give a fuck . . . ? Joel is fine. He sends his regards.

Andy   Bollocks does he.

Angela   Well, don't ask stupid questions then.

Andy   Your kids?

Angela (*pleads*)   Andy?

Andy   Tell me about your kids.

Angela   Micah won another race, four hundred metres. Wants a new pair of trainers.

Andy   Good lad. What else? What else, Ange?

Angela   Natasha has a boyfriend.

Andy   She's eleven.

Angela   You don't have to tell me. He's been round a couple of times, acting like some gangsta in my house. And Joel just stands there, letting it happen.

Andy   He's probably waiting on you.

Angela   He is always waiting on me. Guy can't do one thing for himself. This is no good, I can't do this. Come here.

Andy   I ain't some toy mouse you can wind up, you know.

Angela   Andrew, you want me!

Andy   Yes, I want you, but I can't have you.

Angela   Claire still throwing wobblies? Making you sleep on the couch again?

Andy   You want to help, help me write these reports.

Angela   I'll write you a fucking report for them. Stop sending us more and more bodies, you fucks – there's your report. We got more prisoners than guards. What do they expect? What does Claire expect?

Andy   Me, Ange. She expects me.

Angela   Well, that's me told.

Andy   Yes, cos it's so easy for you to believe that I'm not crazy about you.

Angela   You don't know jack about what I feel.

Andy   Then why do you go back home to him every night?

Angela   You and Claire?

Andy   I'm there for the kids, why do you think?

Angela   You are busting to know if you are better than him in bed?

Andy   You really think that is what this is about?

Angela   Is this a white thing?

Andy   You don't really believe that, do you, Ange?

Angela   Every night when I lay next to him, I shut my eyes and think of you. Happy?

Andy   Then why don't we . . .

Angela   What? What are we going to do, Andrew? Fuck-all is what.

Andy *stops her from leaving.*

Angela   Anyhow, you stop in the middle of it, feeling guilty, I'm going to kill you.

They kiss passionately.

Seven

Angela *is with* **David** *on the landing.*

Angela   So, are you going to keep quiet about this? You going to do this or not?

David   I resent you asking me this, I really do.

Angela   Yes, I think we've established that. You going to do this, yes or no? Look, you're not going to go to hell or nothing if that's what you are worried about?

David   I'm not religious.

Angela   Well, stop acting like a bleeding choirboy then.

David   What's the point in having all these rules if we don't follow them? We're supposed to be better than them.

Angela   Boy, don't lecture me on rules.

David   I think someone has to.

Angela (*chuckles*)   Yer right, yer a not choirboy. You are the governor's illegitimate son, has to be.

David   I heard about this place from everyone; just didn't want to believe it.

Angela   Well, believe it now, boy. Look. You want to do some good, then do it. Do it for me. Nothing is going to come back on you, I swear.

David   Tell that to Johnny Greg.

Angela   Who is Johnny Greg when he's at home?

David   Johnny Greg and I did our training together. Johnny Greg got his first gig at the Scrubs. His first work in, he walks in on his senior officer and two other screws having a 'career chat' with an inmate.

Angela   Where's the shock in that? I've had a few 'career chats' in my time.

David   It was more than that.

Angela   Scrout probably asked for it, mouthing off or summin.

David   They beat everything out of him including the shit. Johnny Greg was asked to turn a blind eye. Johnny Greg was asked to falsify his report. Johnny Greg was asked to lie his arse off in court. Johnny Greg was found guilty of perjury.

Angela   Alright, I get it.

David   He was lucky he didn't get banged up. You want to know where Johnny Greg is right now? Out on a bender with a bottle of JD. That ain't happening to me.

Angela   So, what are you going to do? I need to know, mate, it's only fair. Dave? Ca you know, what happens in the wing, stays in the wing . . .

David   Oh. Don't even bother please, I've heard that.

Angela   Well?

David   If I am ever asked a direct question . . .

Angela   Fair enough.

David   I don't know why you love lying down with them.

Angela   What did you say?

David   They shame you. They shame us.

Angela   How old were you, David?

David   Excuse me?

Angela   A bunch of older black boys used to beat you up when you were a kid, take your pocket money, yeah? How old were you? Ten, eleven? Now you're all grown up, showing some flex. You want revenge, don't you? I bet you tried to join the police? They dash you.

David   You don't know what you are talking about.

Errol *approaches* **Rio** *on the landing.*

Errol   So how you doing, big man?

Rio   You calling *me* big?

Errol   You calling me fat? Ca that would be a huge mistake. I thought it was time I introduced myself. I'm Errol. You could say I am an 'unofficial' designated listener. Speaking of which, are you listening? You better be, cos I ain't got much time.

Rio   Well you best step it up then.

Errol   Young one over there is Saul. He runs this wing. Is this your gear?

Rio   Yeah.

Errol (*points*)   That's Riz. He's one of Saul's boys. When he asks for your gear, give it to him.

Rio   Why would I do that?

Errol   Cos he is the wolf and you are the sheep. He want no trouble from you. Are we clear so far?

Rio   What have people been saying?

Errol   No one bins saying.

Rio   Ca I didn't do it.

Errol   Like I never heard that one before?

Rio   Well, I didn't.

Errol   Not my business what you did?

Rio   I told you I didn't do it.

Errol   I don't need to hear that, blud.

Rio   I'm not yer blud.

Errol   Calm yerself.

Rio   I didn't rape nobody

Errol   Say what?! Say what? You rape – fuck, see, that is exactly what I don't want to hear. It clouds my judgement of you. Get it?

Rio   I don't care how you judge me or not.

Errol   So why you telling me you didn't do it then? Why me?

Rio   Why are you shouting down on me? Are we blood?

Errol   I'm just the listener, I'm nothing to you, you hear me? Nothing! I am here to run you past a couple of things, so don't eat into my time, yeah, otherwise you and me are really gonna fall out. Time is precious, young one, especially as we get so little of it. Feeling me?

Rio   I'm listening.

Errol   Keep it that way. You in hell now, no two ways about it. You live here now.

Rio   That is what the guard said.

Errol   What he told you was official. Now I am about to give you the unofficial. If you wanna be one of those that decides to keep their head down, do yer time, mind yer own business, then that is up to you, no one here is going to stop you from playing that, I'll see to that. But anything you do see – anything – you turn a blind eye. Anything you hear, you go deaf. Screw ask you anything, you don't say shit to them. Follow that, you just might be alright. Shit and shave.

Rio   Say again?

Errol   In and out. Now, if you need anything, make the time go by, you see them. Weed? Skunk? Rent a mobile to call yer mum or gal, Saul's yer man. Whatever you need. But it will cost, much. Newbie's pay up front, no excuses. If you want anything else that isn't as listed, you can still ask, but remember – the bigger the ask, the bigger the task, the bigger the price. Screws here love spinning our cells. They find you with anything you shouldn't have, its solitary time, plus an indefinite loss of privileges. Now I only gonna tell you this once. No matter what these screws might wave at you, you don't say where you got it, ever! Mention Saul's name once and once only, yer dead.

Rio   So, is it alright if I say your name?

Errol   A smart mouth can only get you so far, young one. Might also be wise not to flap your gums about you rape up the poom poom.

Rio   I said I didn't, yeah.

Errol   Don't interrupt me. You go broadcasting it around here like some fucking radio, yer gonna be fighting these brers every day of yer time. You know what they do to a nonce in here? If that happens, if I were you, I would pick one of the hardest brer in here and buss him up, well and truly, take him out. Hear me?

Rio   Seen. I ain't having nobody touching me.

Errol   Saul runs a tip-top wing. Screws love him for it, he gives them an easy life. Follow his rules and for you it's all gravy. So, any questions?

Rio   Why are you telling me all this? Why am I getting the special treatment?

Errol   I'm an old friend of yer mudda's.

Rio   My mum?

Errol   She asked me to keep an eye.

Rio   I don't need a babysitter. She always love to fucking shame me, man.

Errol   Don't speak about yer mudda like that.

Rio   Say what?

Errol   Show some respect.

Rio   Alright, you know what, we're done now.

Rio *does not like the way* **Errol** *is staring at him.*

Rio   You gonna propose? What now?

Errol   You mind what I said.

Errol *leaves.* **Riz** *walks past him as he joins* **Rio** *outside their cell.*

Riz   Gear.

He waits impatiently.

Now.

Rio *hands over his sack.* **Riz** *laughs. He mimics the sound of a sheep in* **Rio***'s face.*

Riz   Yer gonna die here, nonce! (*Calls.*) Saul! Merry Christmas.

Rio *takes the bag over to* **Saul** *and together they share the spoils.*

Riz   Another old film I like is *Lethal Weapon 2*. My fave scene is when Mel Gibson is with Patsy Kensit in 'is trailer, blonde yat from Holby City. She's got all her clothes off, man, lying next to him, her nipples are erect and she's coming out with all kinds of shit, saying they're only up to the fifth inning. See, she's chatting about baseball, but what she really means is that my man Mel must be in good in bed, and he's doing her good, Saul, he's doing her, proper . . .

Angela *approaches.*

Angela   Saul, a word.

Saul (*to* **Riz**)   Go powder yer nose.

Riz (*quotes*)   'Yes, my master'

Errol   Safe.

He stands up.

Saul   Where do you think you are going?

Errol *sits back down.*

Saul   Better.

Saul   You know, you may love to keep up this act of the con who can take everything that's thrown at him, but I reckon, whatever it is that you had, you've used up this to get this far. You grabbing Angie like that proves my point. I don't care what she says, you ain't ready for the outside. You are where I want you, when I want you. Seen?

Errol   Fuck you – in eight weeks, I'm out of this shithole. I have plans.

Saul   What plans?

Errol   My plans.

Saul   Your hustling days are over, nigger.

Errol   I know that.

Saul   You got nuttin out there.

Errol   What have I got in here?

Saul   You got nuff, that is what. The cons like you, I've seen you wid dem. Screws respect you. I could use a man like you working for me. A smart man.

Errol   Where do you think you are, Saul? Where's your suit and tie? I'm done here.

Saul   You'll be banging on the prison door begging them to take you back. I see you. You're the type.

Errol   Not interested.

Saul   Don't hurt my feelings, Errol. I think you should reconsider At the very least, think about it.

Errol   I have thought about it.

Saul   Well, rethink. I insist. Enjoy your book. (*Looks up.*) You still here?

Errol   And stop telling everyone the Trivial Pursuit story.

Saul   I'm just bigging you up, dawg.

Errol   I don't need your help.

Saul   Yer my hero. Come check me in six weeks. I ain't going any place, neither are you.

Errol *goes to his cell.* **Saul**'s *words have obviously got to him as he paces around the room. He eventually stops. He lets out a silent scream then calmly searches for his Trivial Pursuit board game.*

Eight

Errol *is setting up the board for a round of trivial pursuit. Only this time he is playing by himself.* **Angela** *goes into his cell.*

Angela   Could you be any more sad? Isn't there someone you can play with?

Errol   I like playing alone, I do it all the time. Besides, no one wants to play me. I guess they're all tired of having their arses kicked.

Angela   Are you that good?

Errol   Try me.

Angela   I intend to. Sports?

Errol   Shoot.

Angela *picks up a card.*

Angela (*reads*)   Who was the youngest England player before Theo Walcott?

Errol   Wayne Rooney, don't waste my time.

Angela (*reads*)   Who was the first England player to score in three World Cups?

Errol   Beckham!

Angela (*reads*)   Who scored the most goals in the 2004/2005 season . . .

Errol   It doesn't just have to be about football. Thierry Henry, by the way.

Angela (*reads*)   How many miles is the boat race?

Errol   Four. Satisfied?

Angela   Just wait. General knowledge.

Errol   Your time.

Angela (*reads*)   Which day of the week is named after the Roman god of agriculture?

Errol   Saturday.

Angela   What is the world's most southerly ocean?

Errol   The Atlantic Ocean.

Angela   Which country did Christopher Columbus claim Cuba for in 1492. I know this one.

Errol   Oh yes?

Angela   America, innit? Everyone knows that.

Errol   I don't.

Angela   Well, come?

Errol   España.

Angela *reads the answer.*

Angela   Shit!

Errol   I thank you!

Angela   Where did you get a brain so big?

Errol   I paid attention at school.

Angela   Mind you, you've had eight years to learn the answers.

Errol   Why is it so hard for people to consider that maybe, just maybe, I am naturally smart?

Angela   So what you doing here?

Errol   I got caught –

Angela   You got caught, yes! If I was your pad mate, I would have accused you of cheating as well.

Errol   Fancy a game? Try your luck?

Angela   Thanks, Errol, but there aren't enough hours in my day for an arse-whooping.

Errol   Are you fucking him again? Andy. Are you and him fucking again? What is it with white guys like him? Is it one of those 'once you go black, you never turn back' scenarios . . .

Angela   On your feet!

Errol *jumps to his feet.*

Angela   You know, I reckon there should be a question about you in this game. How many times has Errol Kiffin crossed the motherfucking line? Answer, no one knows because they have lost count. You are lucky you are not in hospital for what you did to me, eating through a fucking straw, cos, trust me, Andy wanted to put you there. Why did you do it?

Errol   I was improvising.

Angela   Improvising?

Errol   Throw suspicion.

Angela   You nearly cut my throat.

Errol   I'm sorry.

Angela   For a moment there I thought you was serious.

Errol   Well, that's mad.

Angela   Suicidal more like.

Errol   I wanted my letter.

Angela I've written it. (*Shows him.*) See it deh. Sorry for taking my time, but I have a wing to run.

Errol Saul is offering me his number two.

Angela That motherfucker. I told him.

Errol I can handle him.

Angela So why you shaking?

Errol I just want out of here, Ange. I done my time.

Angela You'll be out soon enough. I've taken care of you.

Errol You're gonna give it to the parole board?

Angela Hold yourself. Now, you take care of me. Give me the name of the screw that smuggled a phone in for Saul.

Errol No way.

Angela We had a deal.

Errol When I am walking out of this wing for the last time, then I'll give it to you, not before.

Angela Don't fuck with me, Errol.

Errol I'm not.

Angela Big mistake.

Errol That name is the only insurance I have that you will play ball.

Angela Don't I always?

Errol Can you say the same for Andy?

Angela I can handle Andy.

Errol The new boy?

Angela You trust me, you trust them.

Errol No.

Angela Errol?

Errol Can't do it.

Angela   Jesus!

Errol   I ain't giving that up. I can't.

Angela   Claart, about you can't!

Errol   In fact, forget what I said, I don't want the letter, I don't want parole. I'm better off here.

Angela   Are you taking the rise here?

Errol   I don't know nothing, I didn't see nothing. Sorry, yeah.

Angela   Have you been got at?

Errol   Please!

Angela   Riz?

Errol   Riz? It's all I can do not to snap his neck.

Angela   I didn't hear that. See to it that I don't not hear it again. What do you want now? Extra privileges. Single cell until you go?

Errol   I'm not giving you the name, Ange.

Angela   Six weeks until your parole hearing, Errol. That's forty-two days of you in my company. And I'm going to enjoy myself. I am going to take my fucking time wid you, cos no one, especially some fucked-up druggie-killing batty bwoi prisoner, is going to make a mug out of me. You are not thinking straight.

Errol   Believe.

Angela *kicks over the board game.*

Angela   You can call that the shape of things to come. I'm going to spin you so many times you are going to get a headache. Clean this mess up. Motherfucker, you are going to give me that name.

Angela *leaves.*

Nine

Errol *steps out onto the landing to see* **Rio** *standing by himself. He strolls over.*

Rio   Why you love to follow me around? You gay?

Errol   This is just a follow up from our last meeting. But if you call me gay again, I'll cut yer throat where you stand.

Rio   I didn't call you gay, I asked if you were gay.

Errol   Is that supposed to make a difference?

Rio   That guy come see me.

Errol   Guy?

Rio   Asian guy, Riz?

Errol   Did you give him your gear?

Rio   I gave it to him. He said I was a nonce, he said I was going to die.

Errol   You best start growing eyes in the back of yer head then.

Rio   That's it?

Errol   Where do you think you are, boy?

Rio   I didn't do it.

Errol   No one cares.

Rio *growls in frustration.*

Errol   Hey, turn that off.

Rio   Fat bitch.

Errol   Hey!

Rio   Well, she is. Or was. Joke is, I only made friends cos I felt sorry for it. She wouldn't stop following me around. One day she is so fat, yeah, she could show up on radar, the next day, she has a Leona Lewis look going on for, telling me how badly she wants it from me.

Errol   She must have really liked you.

Rio   So, why she saying I rape her then? What did she think was going to happen? She should have stayed fat if she didn't want it to happen.

Errol   But you sexed it.

Rio   Course I sexed it. If it's going around for free, you better believe I'm sexing it. With her tight short and short skirt, what did she expect? All of my brers' eyes were on her, it was only a matter of time before they wanted a taste as well, what did she expect, the bitch! Everyone on my estate cussing me, Lester and his boys running me down.

Errol   Who the fuck is Lester?

Rio   You should see him and his boys, strolling round the estate like they're summin.

Errol   Calm down.

Rio   You know what they call themselves? Make you laugh, man, the K–A–P! The 'Kill All Pussies' crew. What kind of shit is that? Fool.

Errol   Kill all pussies?

Rio   Ain't my crew's name.

Errol   What's your crew's name?

Rio   'The Invincible Titans'. T–I–T.

Errol   'Tit'?

Rio   No, T–I–T.

Errol   You call yourselves 'tit'?

Rio   Yu deaf, I said no.

Errol   (*sighs*)   They call themselves 'tit'.

He laughs.

Rio   Wass so funny?

Errol   You don't know, young one, I can't help yer. You, tit!

Rio   Look, you don't know, you weren't there. It's a small estate, can't be helped.

Errol   What you know about DNA, Rio?

Rio   Some.

Errol   They can prove anything. So if you commit a crime and left a bit of yourself, like sweat, tiniest drop, and that's yer arse. So if yu carry on wid this shit about not raping her, yer done.

Rio   Didn't you hear me tell you, I didn't rape her, I sex her.

Errol   What about those other boys? They sex her too?

Rio   Every one of them.

Errol   Yer ejut!

Rio   Ejut? If yer so smart, why are you here?

Errol   Cos I was caught. One don't have anything to do with the other. Everyone is here because they want to be, one way or the other.

Rio   Not me.

Errol   You say that cos yer not thinking.

Rio   I always think.

Errol   Do you ever think about that girl? What's her name?

Rio   I'm done with you sweating me.

Errol   Tell me her fucking name!

Rio   Sasha.

Errol   You ever think about her, Sasha?

Rio   I feel bad, yeah, that it happened.

Errol   Maybe you should feel bad cos it didn't have to happen.

Rio   I don't know why yer so invested in all of this.

Errol   I ought to knock some sense into you. Feel the back of my hand from time to time.

Rio   Excuse?

Errol   Knock some sense into you.

Rio   Who are you, man?

Errol   You have a sister, Rio?

Rio   Why are you interested in me and my family?

Errol   Answer.

Rio   Yeah.

Errol   What if someone did that to her?

Rio   I'd kill him.

Errol   Seen.

Rio   Anyone would. But it weren't rape though.

Errol   Yer telling me, just like that, she just wanted to sex your brers, as well as you?

Rio   Yes.

Errol   Lie!

Rio   I'm not lying.

Errol   You young ones today, man.

Rio   Listen, yeah, save me the old-man-who-is-wise speech, ca I heard it, we've all heard it!

Errol   Get the fuck outta my face, young one – move! You think yer so smart, yu tink yer a bad man, one week in here, let's see how bad. Not a moment's peace, yungsta, every con in here is gonna wanna cut you! Yer gonna fight them all off! You ready for that? Are you? Move!

Rio *has not moved.*

Errol   I said move. What? What? What . . . say summin!

Rio   You're my dad. You are. Aren't you?

Errol (*holds his hand up*)   There was a time, not so long, that you used to fit right here. You had the sweetest laugh, man. No lie. In all of Grove. Look, Rio . . .

Errol *offers his hand.* **Rio** *slaps it away.*

Rio   Stay the fuck away from me.

He goes.

Andy *joins* **Riz** *on the landing.*

Riz (*chants*)   Two–one! Two–one! Two–one! Two–one! . . .

Andy   I don't know why you're chanting. We're the ones who won.

Riz   Yeah, but you still *lost.*

Andy   Ninety-second minute, seconds away from a windfall, no way was that a penalty! No way!

Riz   You lot, wid yer Arsenal and Chelsea, when are you going to understand? Man U are kings and will always be kings.

Andy   Wayne fucking Rooney!

Riz   The force is strong with us.

Andy   Do you have any idea what that ugly little scouse tosspot has cost me? Do yer? That was a blatant bloody dive! Stevie Wonder could have seen that.

Riz   Maybe you should stick with the horses?

Andy   Maybe I ought to take you aside for a little 'career chat'. Eh?

Riz   You look after us, we look after you, remember?

Andy   We'll see you at Stamford Bridge in a few months, shall we, Abdul? Let's see if you are laughing then.

Riz   I would love to stay and chat.

Andy   Me as well.

Riz   You have summin for me?

Andy *waits until there is no one around and as discreetly as possible hands* **Riz** *a mobile phone.*

Andy   Make it count. Tell Saul, as of now, the price has gone up. One of yours has been talking.

Riz   Who?

Andy   Like I said, price has gone up.

Riz (*quotes*)   'You serve your master well. And you will be rewarded.'

Andy   Five minutes.

Riz *leaves.*

Ten

Riz *is in the shower room. He dials a number, then waits.*

Child's Voice (*through receiver*)   Hello?

Riz   Hello.

Child's Voice (*through receiver*)   Who's speaking?

Riz   Is that Anessa or Firyal?

Firyal   Firyal.

Riz   Hello, Firyal.

Firyal   Hello.

Riz   Hello, my darling, how old are you now?

Firyal   Nine.

Riz   Nine! You're nine.

Emily   Who is this?

Riz   I'm your dad . . . Put Mummy on the phone for me, please, will you, sweetheart?

Firyal   OK. Mummy, phone . . .

Riz   (*whispers*)   Daddy loves you.

Yasmin   Firyal, you know you're not supposed to answer the phone, how many more times . . .

Emily   Sorry.

Yasmin   You will be . . . Hello? Anyone there?

Riz   How are you, Yasmin?

Yasmin   Riz? God!

Riz   Firyal sounded big.

Yasmin   And how would you know?

Riz   Answering the phone by herself.

Yasmin   She knows she's not supposed to do that.

Riz   Go easy on her, Yasmin

Yasmin   Was there something you wanted, Riz?

Riz   Say hello.

Yasmin   Well come on, say hello, then go.

Riz   I deserve that.

Yasmin   You deserve more than that.

Riz   You're angry.

Yasmin   You're quick.

Riz   I should go.

Yasmin   You hang up now, don't bother calling me back, ever! I can't keep doing this.

Riz   I'm still hurting you.

Yasmin   Then stop.

Riz   I'll talk to you soon.

Yasmin   Talk to me now.

Riz   Kiss Firyal for me.

Yasmin (*pleads*)   Riz . . .

Riz *hangs up. He wipes his tears.* **Rio** *comes into the room.*

Riz   Yes, what you want? What, what you want?

Rio *clenches his fists.* **Riz** *roars with laughter.*

Riz   Is this joke? Huh? Alright, batty bwoi, come. Come!
Show me what you have?

They circle each other like two boxers in a ring. **Rio** *tries to throw a few punches but misses* **Riz** *each time.*

Riz   Show me what you have. Show me what you have.
Show me what you have. Still waiting, batty bwoi, I say show
me. Yeah. (*Quotes.*) 'The force is with you, young Skywalker.
But you are not a Jedi, yet!'

Rio *growls in anger and runs right at* **Riz** *who overpowers him easily, holds him by the back of the head, putting a knife to his throat.*

Riz   Where the fuck do you think you are, young one? You
think taking me out is going to make your life easier? You
think you can fuck me as easily as you fucked that gal? You
think I'm going to lie down for you? Do you? You are not
going to believe what is happening to you, even when it's
happening. I'm gonna peel you, and yer gonna feel every bit
of it, bitch . . .

Errol *comes in. He rushes* **Riz** *from behind and begins to throttle him with his arm.*

Riz *tries to break free but* **Errol** *continues to squeeze until* **Riz** *gasps his last, dying breath.*

Errol *lays him on the ground.*

Errol (*to* **Rio**)   Go find Andy. Tell him to bring his arse here. Then go back to yer cell. You don't move till I see you. What are you waiting for? Go, go now.

Rio *cannot move.*

Errol   I said go!

Rio *runs out.*

Errol *searches* **Riz**'s *body. He finds the phone, hides it in his pocket.* **Andy** *comes in.*

Andy   Oh Jesus Christ. Jesus Christ, fuck!

He searches frantically for the phone on **Riz**'s *body but cannot find it.*

Errol   Looking for this?

Andy *holds out his hand.* **Errol** *hands the phone to him.*

Andy   Out.

Errol *goes.* **Andy** *speaks into his hand held radio.*

Andy   This is Maggs. I've got an Emergency. Code Red. On the ones, shower room.

Sound of the alarm.

Part Two

One

Angela *enters.*

Angela My husband Joel asked me once, what is it that I fear most about my job. My answer, opening doors. Cell doors to be precise. In the mornings, when they are let out. You see, during the night, when they are all tucked up, it is the only time when we cannot keep an eye on them. They have eight or nine hours alone to do God knows what to each other and to themselves. And believe me they do. We had this one crazy, he strips himself naked, rubs his own faeces and his cellmate's faeces all over his body, before slashing his own wrists with a razor blade. See, his thinking is we would be less likely to try and save him. And he was right, in another life was I going anywhere near him. One of our lot tried, played the hero, he managed to stop the bleeding, that is when he wasn't throwing up every five seconds. In case you are wondering, that prisoner died. And all the Governor cares about is protecting his own arse. Did we do everything we could to save him, did we follow procedure by the book? Never mind that young screw who might have caught God knows what off that man. Now normally when something like that goes down, at the end of the shift we all take each other down to the nearest boozer, knock them back until there's no tomorrow. We keep knocking them back until today's events seem like a vague distant memory in our minds. That's how it go. Screws United! We are there for each other, ca no one is there for us. I shoulda bin larging it with those lot, going blind on double vodkas, but my man Joel has been bitchin it 24/7 lately about how I'm hardly ever home these days. I come home that night to find Joel, sitting on his fat arse again, watching TV with the kids, without it once entering his head to have dinner ready for me. After all his chat. I blow my mates out, for this! That is how much I am valued in my own home. He has the front to ask me how my day was. And he wonders why he hasn't been getting *any* lately. So, I cooked dinner, and waited, until everyone around the table had their mouths full of spaghetti bolognese, when I told them about me seeing a six-foot man killing himself while covered in his own shit that is dripping off him from head to toe. Now who would feel like eating their spaghetti bolognese after hearing a story like that? So, you will understand when I say, me walking into the shower room, seeing a man strangled, all dead up, is no big thing. In fact, it is a luxury.

Two

Andy *enters, followed by* **Rio** *and* **David**.

Rio   He took my gear.

Angela   Is that why?

Rio   He said I was going to die here. I was scared.

Angela   He took your gear, threatened your life, so you strangled him?

Rio   Right!

Angela   You are telling me that is why you did it?

Andy   Ange?

Angela   What?

Andy   You shouldn't be doing this.

Angela   I won't be long.

Andy   Leave it for the police.

Angela   Just a couple more questions.

Andy   They'll be here soon. They're going to go ape shit.

Angela   I want to know what happened!

Andy (*to* **David**)   Are you fucking mute or something now? You got anything to say, choirboy?

David   We are not lawyers, we are not the police. Anything he says here is admissible, as long he repeats it for the old bill.

Angela   You're learning, Smith.

David   Saunders!

Angela   Talk to me, Rio.

Rio   I just did. I don't know why, I just come out of the shower, for some reason he started flexing up on me, giving me a couple of slaps and shit, calling me bitch. Saying that when he gets out, he's gonna find my mum and baby sister, do untold to them.

Angela   Untold what?

Rio   What do you think? He said he was going to make me watch. If I ever survived.

Angela   Survive?

Rio   When he had his back to me, I thought he was reaching for a razor blade that he had hidden. I thought he was going to cut me up. Well, I wasn't waiting. I strangled him. Done deal.

Angela   No, you ain't done, Rio, you are far from done.

Rio   He took my gear.

Angela   You've only been here five minutes. And you don't have the eyes of a killer, man. There has to be a better answer than the one you are giving me.

Andy   Police, Ange?

Angela   Let him talk. Rio?

Rio   He took my gear! It was self-defence.

Angela   You speak like you have that memorised.

Rio   Why can't you believe me?

Angela   Ca yer telling me barefaced lies, that's why?

Andy   Ange?

Angela   What?

Andy   That's enough. David, take him back.

David   Come on, on your feet.

David *takes* **Rio** *out.*

Andy   What is going on with you?

Angela   I want to know what he knows.

Andy   Know what?

Angela   You don't think there is something funny going on here?

Andy   Since when do you give a flying fart?

Angela   Someone died on our watch, Andy. A Muslim! I'm not happy. You telling me that does not mean anything to you?

Andy   They're not paying me enough.

Angela   Something isn't right here.

Andy   What's the worst that can happen? Riz's lot issue fatwa? On who?

Angela   Governor could fire our arses out of here.

Andy   My arse, your arse, whichever, it's never going to happen.

Angela   You Mystic Meg?

Andy   Guvner is a brainless twat, he needs us to run this place. Our job is lock them up and keep them locked.

Angela   Well, we fucked up then.

Andy   What are you so worried for?

Angela   You don't think Saul might have something to do with this?

Andy   Talk to me.

Angela   I had a chat with him, telling him in no uncertain terms not to even think about making Riz number two. He tells me Riz has been stealing from him, and that he was thinking of taking him out.

Andy   So?

Angela   So, this might be him taking him out.

Andy   He steps to a newbie to do it? Don't make sense, Ange.

Angela   Fuck Saul. Fuck Saul, fuck the newbie, I'm worried about me.

Andy   What are you saying?

Angela   I encouraged him, I think my exact words were 'Don't make a mess.' That makes me an accessory in some eyes.

Andy   It does not make you anything, shut up. The kid is giving you a way out here. It happened, just like he said. Go with it.

Angela   But what if it was Saul who –

Andy   Angie, look at me. I'm not letting anything bad happen to you. I won't let it. Ever.

Angela   I should let you go. But I don't want to.

Andy   Then don't.

Three

Angela *is on the landing with* **David***, letting the prisoners out of their cells for association.*

David   How did you end up this way? What happened to you?

Angela   It wasn't just one thing.

David   You're telling me you are not going to miss it – the job, the uniform, all of that power?

Angela   That's the idea.

David   Are you saying that because you believe it, or saying it because you want to believe it?

Angela   You know, for a moment, I thought you were getting it.

David   Getting what?

Angela   You'll learn.

David   Look, if you're trying to prepare me for the rough, don't bother. I'm a big boy. I can handle it. Nothing but a bunch of wrong uns the lot of them, and you get all wound up.

Angela   Don't dismiss them like that, David, they're smarter than that, that would be your first mistake.

David   Your first mistake was that you didn't. You crossed the line and didn't even know it.

Angela   Is that so?

David   Yes, with due respect.

Angela   I wish I could think like you.

David   You should have seen yourself going at Rio. Don't tell me you don't care any more. Don't tell me you're not one of the good guys.

Angela   Are you done?

David   You don't have to leave, Angela. Just do your job.

Angela   Oh, give it a rest, choirboy.

David   Don't let them run you.

Angela   Time for rounds.

David   I'm going by myself?

Angela   You'll cope.

David *goes.*

Rio *passes* **Errol** *on the landing.*

Errol   So, how did it go? Boy, I'm talking to you, how did it go? You told them what I said, yeah? Well, you'll be alright then? Rio?

Rio *shoves* **Errol** *away*

Errol (*chuckles*)   Oh! My feelings are hurt.

Errol *sees* **Saul** *watching them.*

Errol   Go take a walk. Now.

Rio *does as he is told.* **Errol** *wanders over to* **Saul***.*

Saul   What part of 'I want him schooled' did you not understand?

Errol   Why you asking me? I don't even know the boy.

Saul   Everywhere I look, I see you two chatting.

Errol   I'm a listener, aren't I? Riz is gone, what are you crying about?

Saul   I got Angela breathing down, threatening to take away my spot. I'm not fucking happy! I didn't want him dead. Easy life, Errol.

Errol   It will blow over.

Saul   You were supposed to take care of this.

Errol   I didn't say I was going to do it.

Saul   Why didn't you say you was going to use this kid?

Errol   Did you not hear me? I don't know what you are talking about.

Saul   I ask you to get Riz, he gets got, do the math.

Errol   For all I know, you used the kid.

Saul   I'm good, but that not good. How did you get to play him so fast?

Errol   I didn't play anybody Saul, he did it all by himself.

Saul   I wanted you to do it, though.

Errol   Why was that? So, you got summin over me? How stupid do I look, Saul?

Saul   I think I liked you better when you were all quiet and shit.

Errol   I liked me better.

Saul   What's your game, Errol?

Errol   There is no game.

Saul   You think you can rise above me?

Errol   You are getting paranoid in your old age.

Saul   I ain't losing everything I worked for cos of you and some lickle batty bwoi who can't wait to earn his stripes.

Errol   Look, you wanted it done. It was done. 'Don't ask, don't tell.'

Saul   Who is he?

Errol   I have no idea.

Saul   He must want a rep bad. Have a hard on for it. You think we can use him?

Errol   I think he's one of those types, you best leave alone. There is no telling what he might do.

Saul   I'll think it over. Can't say the same for every brer in here, though.

Errol   Even after he took out Riz?

Saul   You married to him or what, Errol? You know how it go in here. Now, I have to go find me a number two. Liam will be a happy man.

Errol   Here's to Liam.

Saul   I ain't losing my spot, Errol. Anyhow, this don't blow over, it's you I'm coming for.

Four

Rio *is in the visiting room with* **Chandra** *and kid brother* **Reece**.

Reece   You only had that yat's number for two minutes, yet there you were, bruv, sending her a text, carrying on like yer loved up or summin, thirty seconds later she's texting you back. Falling for all yer shit. Wouldn't mind so much but I was on it last year, thought she was sweet for me, till you came along.

Rio   Ain't my fault you can't hold yer bitches.

Chandra   Hey!

Rio   What?

Chandra   Watch yer mouth.

Rio   I hope yer bin careful, Reece, don't wind up no baby father.

Reece   No sweat. When you get pussy that fits, you don't run out on it.

Chandra *clouts him.*

Rio   Oh shame, take the blame!

Reece   That bloody hurt, Mum.

Chandra   Just clean out your mouths, both of you. I raised you better than that.

Reece   Rio, she remind me of that one you went wid in school – Tanya, Tina?

Rio   Yer thinking Tiana, but I didn't touch that till after I left school. It was Kisha.

Reece   Kisha, yes! She had that Beyonce look going on for, innit?

Rio   Man, when I think of Beyonce's arse, summin comes outta me. (*Dreamy.*) Ah, Kisha! She was one nasty ho!

Chandra   Rio!

Rio   Have to warn you, Mum, you hit me, they might have to lock you up. In here, they have the same powers as the police.

Reece   You joke?

Rio   For real.

Chandra   Don't encourage him. You are always doing that.

Reece   Why you have to ruin our fun?

Chandra   See me talking to you?

Rio   Nah, Mum's right, shut up. Sorry, Mum. Kisha was a good, nice church girl, Mum. Seriously though, protect yourself with that girl. You know what I'm saying.

Reece   But I hate wearing them, though. Think about it, you get yerself a fine one, nice hottie, yer all over her, got it all going on, then you have to stop and put one on first, that make sense to you?

Rio   Alright, don't wear one. Yer gonna die, though.

Reece   Not everyone dies.

Rio   Just shut up, yungsta, and wear the thing.

Chandra (*snaps*)   Can we talk about something else, please? Do you think it could be at all possible? I mean, can you boys, all of yer, ever talk about anything that isn't to do with sex? Possible? No?

A brief moment of silence for all of them.

Reece   See that Chelsea game, Rio? Sorry, course you didn't.

Rio   Course I did. We do have tele in this place.

Reece   Sky?

Rio   I wouldn't go that far. I saw it on *Match of the Day*.

Reece   So what the fuck was Ashley Cole doing with that backward pass?

Rio   Fool is getting old, he's lost it. Cost us three points.

Reece   His mind just ain't in it.

Rio   I bet I know where his mind was.

Reece   Yeah, too busy thinking about that nice piece of trim he has at home waiting for him.

Rio   Cheryl Cole, definitely.

The boys all clock **Chandra***'s disappointed face.*

Rio   Sorry, Mum.

Reece   Sorry, Mum.

Chandra (*sighs*)   Well, at least you tried.

Rio   You alright, Mum?

Chandra   It's the way people talk about you, son.

Reece   Let them do it in front of me, let them.

Chandra   What is that going to change, Reece?

More uncomfortable silence.

Reece   You make me laugh, Rio. Just get here and already you kill up somebody.

Rio   Didn't mean to.

Chandra   You think this funny?

Rio   No, Mum.

Chandra   I saw your face.

Rio   Mum, I ain't laughing.

Reece   He weren't.

Chandra   I wasn't talking to you.

Reece   You know when yer trial is yet?

Rio   A couple of months from now, they say.

Chandra   We'll be there.

Rio   No, Mum, I don't want to stress you out, you got work and that.

Chandra   You're my son. (*Sighs.*)

Rio   What?

Chandra   Couldn't you have walked away? Couldn't you have done that?

Rio   No.

Chandra   Why not?

Reece   Raghead reached to him, ain't his fault.

Chandra   Reece!

Reece   Well, it ain't.

Chandra   Yes, your brother is a big man.

Reece   What you expect him to do?

Chandra   Believe me I gave up long ago expecting you children to do anything.

Reece   Well, jam yer noise then.

Chandra *clouts him around the head.*

Reece   Don't ever hit me again, Mum.

Chandra   I brought you in this world, I will take you out.

Rio   Hello? You done, remember me?

Angela *approaches.*

Chandra   It's alright. We're alright. (*To her sons.*) Is this the only way to get through to you? What is the matter with you?

Another brief moment of uncomfortable silence.

Reece   I'm headed out.

Rio   Later, Reece.

Reece   Later, bro.

Reece *exits.*

Chandra   What are you trying to do to me? Send me to my grave?

Chandra   He took my gear, Mum, I had no choice.

Chandra   Boy, you always have a choice. There's this guy who in here wid you. His name is Errol. He is an old friend of your dad's.

Rio   And old friend of my dad's?

Chandra   He said he'll keep an eye on you. He promised me. Have you met him yet?

Rio   Yeah, I've met him.

Chandra   Yet this still happened. Why didn't he do something?

Rio   How stupid do you think I am, Mum? Did you honestly think I wouldn't find out? I knew there was summin. From the moment I laid eyes.

Chandra   Baby?

Rio   I didn't need him when I was growing up, I don't fucking need him now.

Chandra   You lower your voice.

Rio   He wants to help, that's his business.

Chandra   I asked him to look out for you.

Rio   Whatever, we have it covered.

Chandra   Have what covered?

Rio   Don't worry yerself.

Chandra   Don't talk to me so. Show some respect! Will it kill you? What has he got you to do?

Rio   What makes you think it's him?

Chandra   Cos I know him. Did you kill that man?

Rio   Yeah.

Chandra   Rio, did you kill that man?

Rio   He took my gear. Why can't you believe me?

Chandra   Cos I know you, and I know yer father.

Rio   So why did you tell him to step to me then?

Chandra   Cos I'm a idiot. Cos I love you, cos I'm worried
for you, cos I'm desperate, alright? Look at me – whatever he
has got you to do, whatever he is asking of you, don't do it.
This is what he does, Rio. He turns his shit on to other people,
so he can get what he wants. All he thinks about is himself.
Whatever he wants you do, don't do it. Tell them the truth.
If you can't tell me, tell them. Rio?

Rio   You know what they do to people like me.

Chandra   But you didn't do that either.

Rio   You think anyone is going to wait to find that out? I ain't
having anyone touching me.

Chandra *begins to cry.*

Rio   Mum, no, come on, man, listen – if yer gonna cry go
outside, I don't want to be seeing this. Go outside, Mum,
please? I'm alright, no one is going to fuck with me, now.

Chandra   You have enough sweets? I'll come again, see you
before the trial.

Rio   Mum?

Chandra   I said I will come.

Angela *leads them out.*

Chandra   All I wanted to do was take him in arms like I
used when he was little, when he was sweet. People stare at
me, like there is something wrong with me, what did I do to
raise a rapist? How can I still love him? What kind of a
question is that? I beg you? You got Errol Kiffin in here?
I wanna see him.

Angela   You can't.

Chandra   I wanna fucking see him, yeah.

Angela   Calm down.

Chandra   Bastard.

Angela   What is it?

Chandra   Bastard!

Angela   Have you finished?

Chandra   Joke is, I never thought I was his type. Never thought for a minute. How right I was.

Angela   I don't get you.

Chandra   Fucker couldn't run fast enough when I told him I was late. Birthday here, Christmas there, whenever he felt like getting laid, that was it. I never asked for anything, never wanted, except this one time! He couldn't even do that. Look after his boy. His own boy.

Angela   Rio?

Chandra   This is not what I wanted. You tell him that for me. You tell that bastard. Please, will you look after him? Look out for him. Whatever it is you do. Please? Reece, come.

Chandra and **Reece** *leave.*

Andy *approaches.*

Andy   Loving mother.

Angela   Fucking skank!

Five

Angela *enters the search room, followed by* **Andy**, *who leads* **Errol** *in.*

Errol   Come on, Ange!

Angela   Stand here.

Errol   What are you doing?

Andy   Just do as she says

Errol *stands where* **Angela** *is pointing.*

Errol   So, what now?

Angela   Don't you move. Look at me. Listen very carefully. Errol Kiffin, you have been brought here because we intend to do a strip search on you . . .

Errol   Say what?

Andy   Ange?

Angela   We have reasons to believe you are hiding something on your person.

Errol   Do I? Is that right?

Angela   We are going to give you clear instructions, you do anything other than what you been asked, and you will be dropped. Do you understand me?

Errol   I understand.

Angela   I told you not to make a mug out of me. Now strip . . .

Before **Angela** *can finish her sentence,* **Errol** *is already taking off his clothes.*

Andy   You know you shouldn't be doing this?

Errol   It's alright, Andy. She must feel like having a real man for a change.

Andy   What did you say?

Angela *strikes* **Errol** *with her baton.* **Errol** *falls.*

Andy   Ange!

Angela   You think I don't know what you are trying to do?

Andy   You can't do that.

Angela   Do you want to wait outside, Andy?

Andy   No, I bloody don't!

Angela   Brer here has been taking me for a fool.

Errol   Your girl is mad, Andy, have a word.

Angela   Was it your idea, Errol?

Andy   Angela, will you talk to me.

Angela   He's the kid's dad.

Andy   What?

Angela   Yes, we have a our own Chris Rock right here. He's got jokes.

Andy   What kid, whose dad?

Angela   Rio, the new boy. He is his dad!

Andy   What?

Angela   Don't you start with you saying bullshit in every sentence.

Andy   Jesus, are you sure?

Angela   You couldn't make that up.

Andy   Right. OK. But I still don't see, Angela, how . . .

Angela   Can't you see what they are trying to do? Kid, yeah, no record of violence at all.

Andy   What?

Angela   If he pleads self-defence, they might believe him. No time added. Laughing boy here on the other hand, ABH, GBH, burglary, assault, possession of a firearm, manslaughter: who would believe him no matter how loud he shouts self-defence?

Andy   The kid is a nonce, Ange. Him and his 'brers' took their turns as well as their time raping that girl. Fuck him! Leave this all to the old bill.

Angela   This is my wing. No one fucks around in it, without my say-so.

Andy   No one is fucking around, Angela. This ain't worth the steam.

Angela   Someone is dead.

Andy   A dope-dealing raghead. The world is a better place without Rizwan in it, Ange. Allah is welcome to him, I won't lose sleep. (*To* **Errol**.) Rio is your boy?

Errol   I didn't know.

Andy   Does he know?

Errol   He does now.

Andy   Jesus Christ.

Angela   How did you do it?

Errol   What?

Angela   Get him to go along with you, so quick? Flex some of that charm of yours on him, Errol? If I was him and I met my dad in here I would have told him to go fuck himself.

Errol   He did tell me that.

Angela   So, how did you do it, Errol?

Errol   I didn't do anything, maybe it happened like the kid said.

Angela   The kid said what? What makes you so sure the kid said anything?

Errol   You said.

Angela   No, I didn't.

Errol   Boy is pleading self-defence.

Angela   No, I said if he pleads self-defence. What makes you so sure he will? Were you there? Errol, I do believe you have fucked yourself.

Errol (*to* **Andy**)   Do you want to control your woman, please?

Angela   You had better start making sense right fucking now.

Errol   You think it was me?

Angela   Yeah, actually.

Errol   Look, he might have done it because I told him to.

Angela   Why would he kill Riz for you?

Errol   He didn't kill him for me.

Angela   You call this making sense, Errol?

Errol   I told him.

Angela   I heard that bit.

Errol   But you're not getting it.

Angela   Enlighten.

Errol   It's my job to tell the new ones how it go. How to survive. One option is to pick a fight with a main man here and buss his arse, and buss it good. That way anyone will think twice about fucking with yer.

Angela   Just like you.

Errol   Just like me. He is in here for rape, Angela. How long do you think he will last once that gets out? I guess he took my advice literally. I come in and saw what he did. I told him to keep saying it was self-defence.

Angela   You feed him that? That was your brilliant master plan?

Errol   Look at me however you want to, but I saved that boy's life.

Angela   Saved his life? You might as well have pulled the trigger, Errol. I don't believe you.

Andy   It sounded good to me, Ange.

Errol   Yes, listen to yer man here.

Angela   I reckon you killed Riz. And you are using this boy, your own son, to cover your arse.

Errol   Why would I kill him?

Angela   Orders from Saul.

Errol   I don't take orders from that bitch.

Angela   You're as frightened of him as anyone else. You will do almost everything to get parole.

Errol   Yeah, well, it ain't what you know, it's what you can prove.

Angela   You seriously want to take that kind of chance with the police? Why don't you make this easy for yourself? None of this needs to go any further.

Errol   Here we go.

Angela   Give me the name of the bent screw.

Errol   Like a dog with a bone!

Angela   If you want me to go along with this, you better cough it up. Just gimme it, why you holding onto it for? Gimme!

Errol   Bitch, don't ever lay yer finger on me again.

Andy   Alright, step back, Kiffin.

Errol   Best tell her.

Andy   Step back.

Angela   Gimme the name.

Andy   Ange, will you just think this through for a second, please? You have got nothing to threaten him with. Not unless you want to implicate yourself – remember your chat with Saul? Come on, girl, just go with it.

Angela   Wipe that fucking smile right off, Errol.

Errol   I weren't smiling.

Andy   Come on, Ange.

Angela   Get off me.

Andy   Come on, just leave it.

Angela   You say I got nothing, Andy?

Andy   Just leave it, will yer!

Angela   But all I have to do is drop the heaviest of hints to Saul about him being a snitch, and never mind six weeks, this one won't last six minutes.

Andy   You are one stubborn bitch, you know that?

Angela   How you feel about that, Errol?

Errol   I don't business about Saul, bring him, let's have it.

Angela   Then there's Rio.

Andy   Ange?

Errol   Say again?

Angela   I said Rio, you deaf?

Errol   Nuh.

Angela   Nuh what?

Errol   You wouldn't.

Angela   I wouldn't?

Errol   He's only a boy.

Angela   You're the one who dragged him into this.

Errol   You know what they will do to him.

Angela   I can imagine.

Errol   Come on, Ange.

Angela   Yes, dog, beg!

Andy   Don't do this.

Angela   I'm not, he is.

Errol   Sick joke, this.

Angela   Who says I'm joking?

Errol   We both know you don't have the heart for that.

Angela   You have no idea what I could do.

Errol   But he ain't done nuttin.

Angela   That's for starters. Keep going.

Errol   Alright, it was me that did Riz. Alright. Just like you say. I told him to say it was him, so I could get parole, I played him, my own son – are you happy now?

Angela   Still waiting on my main course, Errol.

Errol   Come on, Ange.

Angela   Fuck 'Come on, Ange'! Talk to me. Talk to me. Gimme the fucking name!

Errol   You know, just might yu nuh, might be worth it to see the look on your face.

Angela   What does that mean? You want Rio hurt?

Andy   Stop it, Ange.

Angela   You want him in pain?

Errol   You won't rise to that. You can't.

Angela   I'm gonna make your boy's life so unbearable –

Errol   You won't.

Angela   Whatever Saul wants with him,

Errol   You fucking won't.

Angela   I will turn a blind eye to it so many times –

Errol   No.

Angela   I'll lose count. You think I won't do it!

Errol   No!

Angela   I will do it, Errol! I will do it.

Errol   Yer in the shit too.

Angela   Is that right?

Errol   I'm not talking to you.

Angela *realises who he means. She faces* **Andy**.

Andy   What? What? Why couldn't you leave well enough alone?

Errol   So, are we done now? We done? Earth calling Ange –

Angela   Get out.

Errol *leaves.*

A tense silence follows.

Andy   Don't look at me like that, Ange, you're breaking my heart. Don't look at me like that. It was only a couple of phones. As long as it keeps them quiet; easy life, Ange!

Angela   We own them, they don't own us. You told me that.

Andy   Look . . .

Angela (*rages*)   You! Fucking horses, wasn't it?

Andy   Last Grand National cleared me out. I've been robbing Peter to pay Paul ever since. Claire is threatening to leave, take the kids. She's serious this time. We've barely got enough food on the table.

Angela   You couldn't come to me?

Andy   With what? A couple of phones, I swear to you. They were paying me good money. They are getting theirs, I am going to get mine.

Angela   Did you have anything to do with this?

Andy   Like what?

Angela   Tell me.

Andy   Errol told me what happened. He had to, Riz had one of the bloody phones with him.

Angela   You took it?

Andy   No, Ange, I left it on him.

Angela   Don't get lippy.

Andy   I'm the senior officer, in case you've forgotten.

Angela   You think now is the time and place to pull rank? You are removing evidence from a crime scene.

Andy   What evidence?

Angela   Now you sound like them.

Andy   I will never be like them. I know where the line is.

Angela   You have just crossed the bloody line. They own you.

Andy   I was losing my family.

Angela   You fucking gambler, you fucking addict!

Andy   You going to tell?

Angela   It breaks my heart that you even have to ask. That's twice in the space of five minutes you've done that. Do you even care about that?

Andy   Of course I care.

Angela   All you care about is yer next race. That you ain't getting no more trim.

Andy   Don't say that.

Angela   Where's the phone?

Andy *hands it to her.*

Angela   You kept it on you?

Andy   I was going to sling it.

Angela   You are stupid. Everything about you is stupid.

Andy   The way I feel about you isn't stupid.

Angela   Yes, good one, Andrew, yer up shit creek and you want to talk about sex.

Andy   You think that is what I'm doing?

Angela   I don't care what you do.

Andy   I don't care either. They can arrest me, send me back here as a prisoner, whatever! All I care is that I let you down.

Angela   Don't.

Andy   Don't what, tell you how I feel?

Angela   I'm leaving.

Andy   Leaving?

Angela   I'm hanging up my uniform.

Andy   You never said. Why?

Angela   Cos I can't take this job any more, I hate it. I hate it.

Andy   You can't go.

Angela   It is shit, infectious shit. Look who I am talking to.

Andy   How many passes in the visiting room have we turned a blind eye to?

Angela   We are not their mules, we don't bring it in for them. You broke the rules. David told me he wants to do good here. I can't remember what that felt like.

Andy   So, what now?

Angela   I'm going to pass that letter of recommendation to the parole board for Errol. Cos I want that fucker out of here, pronto. The sooner he is someone else's problem, the better. Then I'm going to go home and kiss my babies.

Andy   What am I going to do?

Angela   Thank yourself lucky you still have a job.

Andy   Ange?

Angela   I can't help you, Andy.

Andy Ange?

Angela Let me go.

Six

Errol *is with* **Rio** *on the landing.*

Errol Normally what you do is get a kiss from yer girl, on
the lips, mouths open, like yer doing a French. Now if yer girl
is smart, she's got it wrapped up tight and small in cellophane,
and held up in her mouth, so when she's lipsing you, you pass
it over. Now, if you have a good screw on duty in the visiting
room like our Ange, she can turn around, giving you just
about enough time to get it down yer pants, in yer arsehole,
right up yer arsehole, you bottle it, that's what it's called. But
it is an awkward little manoeuvre, very awkward indeed.
You're against the clock, so I thought, fuck it, I will just cheek
it. Get it down there, hold it tight between the cheeks as I
walk. So I've cheeked it, then they do the usual, legs apart, pat
me down. Fucking thing only dropped out from between my
cheeks and rolled down my trousers leg, didn't it? So it rolled
out, I'm the box, getting padded down, and it has just
dropped . . .

Rio Plopped?

Errol Right on the box. So the screws have looked at me,
and I've looked at them, and I goes, 'Alright, guv?' The
screw's going, 'Errol, Errol, we're gonna nick yer, Errol.' I'm
going, 'Alright, guv, easy, guv,' and hear what, they let me go.

Rio You lie!

Errol Ask me why?

Rio Why?

Errol Cos they know I never give them no grief. I was an
altar boy. The look on that screw's face, he was more surprised
than me.

Rio   Don't know why you're telling me.

Errol   Thought it might help.

Rio   I don't smoke weed.

Errol *looks surprised.*

Rio   I don't! It's bad for my sinuses.

Errol   Right, I won't be keeping yer. Best be gone before they change their mind about letting me out. See you out there one day, yeah? Keep yer pecker up.

Rio   I don't do pills either.

Errol   You might want to reconsider.

Rio   Why?

Errol   They can help you.

Rio   For what?

Errol   To forget.

Rio   Mum said I should stay away from you.

Errol   She's about to get her wish.

Rio   She says you used me.

Errol   I did.

Rio   Why!

Errol   Why do you think? To get out.

Rio   Yer a bastard, man.

Errol   I've been called worse

Rio   Mos def!

Errol   You started this, when you decided to go all Jason Bourne on Riz.

Rio   You told me to.

Errol   I advised you. You decided when, you decided who. That shit is all on you, little man.

Rio   Why did you help me? Why didn't you just let Riz finish me off?

Errol   Go cry somewhere else.

Rio   Why? Say it.

Errol   Say what?

Rio   You know what . . .

Errol   I'd knock that shit off if I were you, blud.

Rio   Too scared to say it, too scared to mean it, innit, Errol?

Errol   It was self-defence. Keep saying that, you'll be fine. The word is spread that you did Riz. It won't stop every ejut from taking a pop at yer, but they'll think twice.

Rio   Thanks, *Dad*!

Errol   I bet you want to hit me. I bet you are bursting to gimme a right caning. Come on then, hit me? See if I don't wipe the floor of the whole wing with yer face. Don't ever think I won't. I have plans, young one, none of them include you. Why you have to come here? Break your mudda's heart? To do what, follow after me? Why don't you tell me the truth about what happened with that girl? Admit what you did.

Rio   I don't owe you anything.

Errol *grabs* **Rio***'s arms.*

Rio   Get that off me.

Errol   Think I'm playing?

Rio   I don't owe you.

Errol   That's not why I am asking.

Rio   Step out of my range, Errol.

Errol   You ain't moving till you answer my question.

Rio   Move!

Errol   Answer me!

Rio   You seriously think now is the time to step up, be my dad? That time has gone, you missed it.

Errol   Answer my question.

Rio   No.

Errol   Not one fucking step, Rio. Know I ain't joking.

Rio   You really wanna! You really wanna know, do yer? All I did was like her, I liked her, and she liked me. She was funny, made me laugh, could cuss like a brer. She wanted to make herself look tic for me. And she was, everyone at that party was bigging me up. But my brers just wouldn't leave her alone, leave us alone. 'Share the taste blud, share the taste,' on and on! There was four of them, they wouldn't let us leave. I thought they were my brers. She wouldn't stop crying. I told her, it will be alright, it'll be alright. Just shut yer eyes, and think that it is me. What you think they would have done to her if they had to force her to do it? What do you think they would have done to me if I tried to stop them? I thought they were my brers, alright!

Errol   You gave her to them?

Rio   I had to. What could I do? You hate me? She does, that's why I'm here. You sorry you stopped Riz from cutting me? Are you? Well, I don't business, you understand? I ain't having no one who don't know me trouble me.

Errol   Do you have any idea how long you have to keep this hard man act up?

Rio   As long as it takes.

Errol   As long as it takes? This is it young one, for ever.

Rio   Fine. Bring it. What? What's that look for, what?

Errol   Tell them the truth about Riz.

Rio   Say what?

Errol   Tell then what really happened.

Rio   No.

Errol   Save yourself, Rio.

Rio   I thought I was.

Errol   You are not cut out for this, it's written all over.

Rio   What about you?

Errol   What about me?! You don't know me. Like you say, I used you. My own blood.

Rio   Think I don't know that?

Errol   So what you doing here? Go tell them.

Rio   No.

Errol   No?

Rio   I'm not like you.

Errol   So what, yer gonna stay in jail just to spite me? Yer soff!

Rio   You tell them. If you're desperate for them to know the truth, you tell them. Tell them. Well, what are you waiting for Errol? Fucking tell them. Be a man for once, be my dad!

Errol *does not move.* **Rio** *shakes his head in utter disappointment.*

Rio   Mos def!

He leaves.

Angela *is with* **David** *on the landing.*

Angela   Look, Saunders, I ain't got time for you, alright?

David   Now you remember my name.

Angela   Just let me enjoy my last shift and I'm out of your life.

David   I'm sorry.

Angela   Why?

David   I just am.

Angela   This will all be yours soon.

David   They won't know what's hit them.

Angela   I hope so.

David (*surprised*)   What?

Angela   Like you said, nothing but scum.

David   Are you winding me up?

Angela   Good luck to you, (*joking*) *Sanders*!

David *chuckles.* **Angela** *leaves.*

Seven

David *brings* **Saul** *into the search room.*

Saul   So, what I can do you for, brother?

David   You will address me as Mr Saunders, Guv or Sir, it's your choice.

Saul   What can I do you for, Mr Saunders . . . ?

David   You speak when I tell you to. Now – (*Recites.*) You have been brought here because I intend to perform a strip search on you . . .

Saul   Oh, come on.

David   I have reasons to believe you are hiding something on your person.

Saul   Don't do this.

David   I am going to give you clear instructions. You do anything other than what you have been asked and you will be dropped.

Saul   Look, Angela, Andy and me had an understanding.

David   Do you understand me?

Saul   They allow the occasional pass as long I don't take the piss.

David Do you understand me?

Saul What do you think will happen if the cons don't get the occasional high? You'd have a riot on your hands, blud, every week? You need me.

David New rules. You are no longer top dawg. As of now, you are all cons. No more career chats, no more turning blind eyes. Make me happy, you get a treat. Make me upset, you get nothing. That is it. Easy life. You follow me? Now, take your fucking clothes off.

Saul Was this Errol's doing?

David Right now.

Saul It was! Tell that nigger from me, he better pray our paths never cross again!

David Clothes!

Saul *takes off his clothes.*

Saul You, are making a serious mistake, my brother.

David You're no brother of mine. You shame me. You shame us.

Eight

Errol *is with* **Angela**.

Angela One gold watch. Is that a Cartier?

Errol Better believe.

Angela Jesus.

Errol You want it?

Angela *glares at him.*

Errol For real, Ange, what?

Angela (*continues*) One black wallet.

Errol *opens it.*

Angela   It's all there.

Errol   Just checking, in case you've given me back too much. Joke!

Angela   Sign here.

Errol   Is that it, then?

Angela   Not unless you want to stay. I don't ever want to see your fucking face again.

Errol   Look after the boy for me, Ange.

Angela   Yes, cos that should be my mission in life.

Errol   Say what?

Angela   Are you still here?

Errol   Don't be like that.

Angela   If he's brave enough to go at it with Riz, he don't need looking after.

Errol   This is my boy here, Ange. You didn't mean what you said. You got the screw's name, you got Andy. A deal is a deal.

Angela   You will have to take it up with the next man.

Errol   Next man? You are the man.

Angela   I'm leaving too, Errol.

Errol   No, you're not.

Angela   My final shift ends in exactly an hour.

Errol   You can't.

Angela   I am done with you niggers, well and truly.

Errol   Rio, Ange?

Angela   What about him?

Errol   Tell me what are you doing for him? (*Shouts.*) Just tell me!

Angela (*calls*)   Andy, you have a minute?

Andy *approaches.*

Errol   Alright, you don't need to do that, yeah, peace. I just want to know what you are doing for my boy?

Andy   I'm sure Saul can find a place for him?

Errol   Saul? Wid you running tings? (*To* **Angela**.) Ange, for fuck's sake.

Angela   If you don't mind, Errol, we would like you to leave.

Errol   But he knows, this fool here knows about me and you.

Angela   Step back.

Errol   How do I know he can keep his mouth shut?

Angela   You don't.

Errol . What the fuck does that mean, 'You don't'?

Andy   Calm it, Errol.

Errol   You move away from me.

Angela   You are not my problem any more.

Errol   This ain't about me, it's about Rio.

Angela   Who's a grown man.

Errol   Saul will eat him alive. But that's nothing compared to what he will do if he ever finds out about me.

Angela   Well, you better hope he never does.

Errol   This is not what I wanted.

Angela   You in jail. Who says you must have what you want?

Andy   On your way now, Errol. Let's be having you.

Errol *shoves* **Andy** *off him.*

Angela   Errol, what are you doing?

Errol   You know you can do summin. Why can't you do it?

Angela   Because our job is to lock you up, nothing else. Yes, Andrew?

Andy   Completely.

Angela   Now fuck off.

Errol   I'm not going.

Angela   Oh yes you are.

Errol   You think I'm shit, I don't blame you. Fair do's.

Angela   All of yer, nothing but fucks.

Errol (*pleads*)   Ange, please, I can't do this!

Angela   Are you scared? You should be.

Errol   I ain't going.

Andy   Now?

Angela   As good a time as any.

Andy *grabs* **Errol** *from behind.* **Errol** *struggles and manages to break free several times before* **Angela** *lands him a blow at the back of the knee.* **Errol** *collapses.* **Angela** *and* **Andy** *both hold his arms over each of their shoulders and take him to the exit door, where they dump him outside and lock the door behind him.*

Errol *struggles to get to his feet and eventually does. He looks up and realises he is out. He looks terrified and begins banging on the door, but no one will answer.* **Errol** *stops and lets out a huge piercing scream.*

Kwame Kwei-Armah

Seize the Day

'How have we come to be mere mirrors to
our own annihilation? For whose entertainment
shall we sing our agony? In what hopes?'

Ayi Kwei Armah, *Two Thousand Seasons*

'As of 2008, forty per cent of London's total population
was from an ethnic minority group.'

londoncouncils.gov.uk

'Across London, black and Asian children outnumber
white British children by about six to four.'

Daily Telegraph, 7 June 2008

Kwame Kwei-Armah

Kwame Kwei-Armah won the Peggy Ramsay award for his first play, *Bitter Herb* (1998), which was subsequently put on by the Bristol Old Vic, where he also became writer-in-residence. He followed this up with the musical *Blues Brother, Soul Sister* which toured the UK in 2001. He co-wrote the musical *Big Nose* (an adaptation of *Cyrano*) which was performed at the Belgrade Theatre, Coventry, in 1999. In 2003 the National Theatre produced the critically acclaimed *Elmina's Kitchen* for which in 2004 he won the *Evening Standard* Charles Wintour Award for Most Promising Playwright, and was nominated for a Laurence Olivier Award for Best New Play 2003. *Elmina's Kitchen* has since been produced and aired on Radio 3 and BBC4. His next two plays, *Fix Up* and *Statement of Regret*, were produced by the National Theatre in 2004 and 2007. He directed his most recent play, *Let There Be Love*, when it premiered at the Tricycle Theatre, London, in 2008. He received an honorary doctorate from the Open University in 2008.

Seize the Day was first performed as part of the 'Not Black and White' season at the Tricycle Theatre, London, on 22 October 2009. The cast, in order of appearance, was as follows:

Jeremy Charles	Kobna Holdbrook-Smith
Sam	John Boyega
Lavelle	Aml Ameen
Howard Jones	Karl Collins
Susan	Sharon Duncan-Brewster
Jennifer Thompson	Jaye Griffiths
Ravinder Persaud	Abhin Galeya
Alice Charles	Amelia Lowdell
Sheila	Cecilia Noble

Director Kwame Kwei-Armah
Designer Rosa Maggiora
Lighting Designer James Farncombe
Sound Designer Tom Lishman
Costume Supervisor Sydney Florence
Production Manager Shaz McGee
Casting Suzanne Crowley and Gilly Poole
Video Design Dick Straker for mesmer
Associate Video Design Ian Galloway for mesmer

2009/10 new writing for new audiences
supported by BLOOMBERG

Characters

Jeremy Charles, *former insurance executive, now a celebrity. Male, mid-thirties*

Lavelle, *urban youth, seventeen*

Howard Jones, *head of major statutory organisation. Male, late forties*

Jennifer Thompson, *head of organisation 'Campaign Black Vote'. Female, thirties*

Alice Charles, *Jeremy's wife. White female, thirties*

Ravinder Persaud, *MP and close friend of Howard. Asian male, very late thirties*

Susan, *close friend to Jeremy. Female, late twenties*

Sheila, *Lavelle's mother. Female, late thirties*

Sam/Assistant, *male, twenties*

Act One

Scene One

THE DAY BEFORE *is projected on to the back wall.*

Westfield Shopping Centre. We cannot see the **Cameraperson**, *just hear her voice. Standing in front of the camera, fixing his tie, is* **Jeremy Charles**: *thirty-five, good-looking, well-spoken star of a TV reality show, now turned presenter.*

Jeremy   Collar OK?

Cameraperson   Shirt wouldn't be my choice of colour but . . .

Jeremy (*playing*)   When I want your sartorial opinion I'll ask . . . Alright, ready to go.

Cameraperson   Turning.

He puts on his 'smiley', nearly over-the-top TV-personality face.

Jeremy   I'm here at the Westfield Shopping Centre . . . and I have to tell you it's every woman's dream and every man's –

A young black male, **Sam**, *early twenties, walks directly in front of the camera and approaches* **Jeremy**.

Sam   Hey? Ain't you the guy from the telly? Don't try and avoid my gaze, bruf, I know it's you. You were wicked on that *Apprentice*-like ting. My mum *loves* you. Trus!

Jeremy   Well, tell her hello for me.

Sam   Wait, does that mean that I'm on da telly?

Jeremy (*trying his best to be polite*)   Is it possible we could have this conversation once I've –

Sam   When's it out blud, tonight? In fact, how you get into this telly ting? All my friends say I could be famous, you know . . .

Jeremy (*gently, politely*)   Really? I'll speak to you about that just as soon as I've finished this take?

Sam   Of course. Love da TV talk. Take, you know.

He moves off. **Jeremy** *looks to camera and smiles; this has happened many times before.*

Jeremy   OK, we good?

Cameraperson   Turning.

Jeremy   I'm here at the Westfield Shopping Centre. And I have to tell you it's every woman's dream and every man's fantasy to have –

We hear a God-almighty noise from off camera. Shouts and screams. **Jeremy** *turns to see what's happened. A group of three or four young people, black and white, have thrown a* **Young Man** *up against a shop window, and it looks as if they are mugging him, stripping him of his clothes. The young man screams.*

Young Man   I ain't got nothing, bruf, I ain't got nottin! I didn't do it, trust!

Lavelle   Shut your mouth. You wanna get shank? Is that it, bruf? Is it?

Jeremy, *automatically shouts out as he sees the youth open his jacket as if to pull out a knife. The camera stays on.*

Jeremy   Ehhh!

Cameraperson (*as if to stop him*)   Jeremy!

Jeremy *runs towards the group. The camera moves forward a little but stays well back, capturing the action on a zoom.* **Jeremy** *arrives at the group.*

Jeremy   Come on, guys, what is this? Leave the boy alone, what's wrong with you . . . ehhh!

He is just about to pull the young people off –

Yo! Come on . . .

– when **Lavelle**, *seventeen, pulls out his knife and swipes it towards* **Jeremy**. *It's clear, however, he isn't aiming to cut him.*

Lavelle   Step back, old man? This ain't got nothing to do with you. Move!

Jeremy   What?

Lavelle   I said move!

This time, however, the youth moves the knife as if he is about to stab **Jeremy**. *Without thinking,* **Jeremy** *slaps the boy in his face with all his might. He was not being a hero, just his natural reaction. The camera zooms in on* **Lavelle** *on the ground, blood pouring from his mouth. It almost repeats the image a few times, before the projection fades on a frame of* **Jeremy**, *almost smiling.*

Lights.

Scene Two

A week or so later.

Office of **Howard Jones**, *head of a major statutory organisation, very late forties.*

Jeremy *is sitting by himself. We hear the sound of a fly buzzing around him. At first he waves it off. After three or four attempts he decides it must die. He waits, two hands open, for the fly to get within range.*

Howard *enters.*

Howard   So sorry to have kept you –

Jeremy *silently indicates that* **Howard** *should stand still. After a beat or so* **Howard** *hears the fly too.*

Clappp! **Jeremy** *slams his hands together. When he opens them, the fly is there.*

Jeremy   Got ya! And it's not even dead.

Howard   Very impressive.

Jeremy   Sorry about that. May I?

Jeremy *goes to the window to release it.*

Howard   Of course.

He does. We hear it fly away. **Howard** *takes out a bottle of antibacterial hand lotion and offers it.*

Jeremy (*taking it*)   Oh, thank you.

Now that **Jeremy**'s *hands are clean,* **Howard** *offers his.*

Howard   Howard Jones, Head of the Commission for –

Jeremy   I know who you are, sir. It's a pleasure to meet you.

Howard   No, no, the pleasure is all mine. When I told my children that I was seeing you today they all got terribly excited. As did my ex-wife. You were wonderful in that show, by the way.

Jeremy   You saw it?

Howard   Oh, I never missed an episode. Gotta keep up with what's happening in the world of reality TV, especially when our people's involved, right? Sit down.

They do.

So you're causing a bit of a storm at the moment, aren't you?

Jeremy   If you're speaking about the suspension . . .

Howard   No, I'm speaking about the thousands of letters to the BBC protesting against it. And the hundreds of letters in the papers and blogs proclaiming you a hero.

Jeremy   I wouldn't read that stuff . . .

Howard   You should. It's all very complimentary. You have done well. Are you married, Jeremy?

Jeremy   Yes, yes, I am.

Howard   Children?

Jeremy   Regretfully, no.

Howard   Don't regret, it's a good move. Terribly expensive children. My daughter thinks Gucci is her middle name. Anyway . . .

He smiles at **Jeremy**. *Then leans back in his chair.*

Howard   Thank you so much for coming in to see me.

Jeremy   As I said, my pleasure.

Howard   So, of course we all know you'll be reinstated, but what are your plans, say they don't?

Jeremy   I'd just go back to selling insurance.

Howard   You don't have to be humble with me, Jeremy, you were one of AIG-UK's top brokers.

Jeremy   Those were the days, eh!

Howard moves into super charm mode.

Howard (*like a new idea*)   You interested in politics at all, Jeremy?

Jeremy   Yeah, a little . . .

Howard   A little? Why a little?

Jeremy   Suppose if you don't get involved, what right do you have to complain when things go wrong.

Howard   I agree, good.

Although answering, **Jeremy** *is scanning hard to work out the agenda of the meeting.* **Howard** *is scanning too.*

Howard   I suppose you're wondering why I've asked you here?

Jeremy   Sorry, was I giving that off? My wife always says I give off what I'm thinking.

Howard   We should have a game of poker sometime then. .

Jeremy   I don't gamble.

Howard (*checking further*)   You a drinking man?

Jeremy   No. I don't smoke either. (*Then, trying to loosen up the vibes.*) But I love me some loose women.

Howard   Really?

Jeremy   I was kidding.

Howard   You Muslim?

Jeremy   No, just didn't like the taste of alcohol as a kid and never made it to the smoke thing.

Howard   Not even a little ganja ?

Jeremy   Especially ganja. Too many where I grew up went crazy on that stuff. Na, not for me.

Howard   You're a little angel then, aren't you?

Jeremy   I wouldn't say that . . .

Howard   No, no, no, no, don't step back from it . . . it's good, very, very good. Me, I'm afraid, can't resist a good claret, Havanan cigars – and loose women, alas, my days of attracting them have long passed.

Jeremy   You're still quite a good-looking man. What are you, fifty?

Beat, as **Howard** *turns dark momentarily, taking umbrage at the age comment for a millisecond.*

Howard   Forty-seven. However, some might say slapping young boys in shopping centres and smiling about it might be a slight character flaw.

Jeremy   . . . I didn't smile.

Howard   The last frame definitely looked like a smile to me.

Jeremy   I was trying to protect myself. There was such fear in that young man's eyes, that I was about to be – *(stabbed)*.

Howard *(ignoring)*   Fine, fine, fine. Look, here's the rub. The people liked you before – now they positively love you. You may wonder what that has to do with me. Well, I'm looking for someone that can chime with the general public . . .

He leaves it hanging.

Jeremy   To?

Howard   Run for public office.

Jeremy   Which one?

Howard   Mayor of London.

Jeremy *laughs.*

Howard   Why you laughing? This is deadly serious.

Jeremy   And are you asking me if I'd like to . . .

Howard   Yes! Boris has just shown us that you can just walk off the street and step into the second most powerful position in the country.

Jeremy   Why aren't you going for it then? (*Leans back.*)

Howard   Everyone wants to be opening batsman. You, my son, are Gary Sobers and Brian Lara rolled into one.

Jeremy *chuckles.*

Howard   I see you like the cricketing metaphor.

Jeremy   I'd have preferred Mohammed Ali and Mike Tyson but I'll accept the compliment with the grace it was given.

Howard (*new idea*)   What percentage of the population of London would you say is ethnic?

Jeremy   I don't know . . . twenty? (*Shrugs his shoulders.*)

Howard   Forty per cent! And they reckon that by the time of the next mayoral elections it could be closer to forty-five.

Jeremy   I didn't know that . . .

Howard   No, you didn't, did you. But with what you have – with the correctly placed articles, right TV appearances behind you – we could harness your natural crossover appeal and have the white community eating out of our hands. And maybe, just maybe, we could have a mayor that looks like me or you. Wouldn't that be fun?

Jeremy *doesn't respond.*

Howard   You're doing that thing with your face again . . .

Jeremy   So you're asking me because I'm black?

Howard (*jumps straight in*)   Nooo! Well, not totally . . .
(*Charms.*) The mayor chair is for everyone. It's just that it's not
one that *we* have sat on before . . .

Jeremy   There's only been two . . . .

Howard   And the third could be you . . . I don't know
about you, but my parents would smile in their graves at the
thought of a black Mayor of London. Wow! Look, this is a
huge thing to just throw at ya. Go home and think about it.
Of course this conversation is strictly Chatham House. You
can't tell anyone.

Jeremy   I understand. Thank you for, um, thinking of me.
I'll get back to you . . .

Howard   Are you at least interested?

Jeremy   Yeah . . .

They get up to leave the office.

Howard   You mustn't underestimate the power you have
right now. (*Leading him.*) There's a Latin phrase for this
moment . . .

Jeremy   *Carpe diem.*

Howard   Seize the day. Make sure you do. Good.

The fly returns and starts buzzing around. **Howard** *immediately goes
for the kill and gets the fly with his first clap. He puts it in the bin and
wipes his hands with his gel.*

Jeremy   Impressive.

Howard   As are you, Mr Charles. As are you.

Lights.

Scene Three

Susan's *house.*

Candles, low lights. **Susan** – *late twenties, black, fine, in very few clothes* – *hears the bell ring. She jumps up and opens the door. Enter* **Jeremy**. *Without letting him speak, she greets him with a long passionate kiss.*

Susan   Hey, baby, how's your day been?

Jeremy   Nothing out of the ordinary – you?

She heads off to the kitchen.

Susan   Bastard of a day. One of the tenants – well, former tenants – arrived back from Kenya to find out that he'd been evicted and demanded to see the head of the org. I came downstairs all hard and ready to tell him he was the one that disappeared for two years. But when he saw me he just broke down in tears and cried like a child. He just kept on screaming, 'The pictures of my children, of my dead mother have been destroyed . . .'

Jeremy   Really?

Susan   I just sat there and cried with him, knowing that there was nothing I could do. A beautiful man to look at . . .

Jeremy   You take too much of that stuff on board, you know, Suz.

Susan (*playful*)   I know . . . That's why I called you round, so you can sweet me up.

Jeremy   Stop that dirty talk!

Susan   That's why you love me, isn't it?

She starts to feed him.

Jeremy   I'm a big boy now, you know, I can feed myself!

Susan   I know. But I bet she doesn't do this.

He stares at her.

Jeremy   You are such a beautiful woman, Susan, you know that?

Susan (*playing with him*)   Tell me again.

Jeremy (*says it exactly the same*)   You are such a beautiful woman, Susan, you know that?

Susan   No tell me again.

Jeremy   Shuddup.

They laugh.

Susan   That's better, you done.

She puts some food in his mouth and then kisses it.

Jeremy   You not eating?

Susan   No. Tell me about yours.

He doesn't speak.

J, I said what happened in your day?

He does not reply.

Susan   It's you I'm talking to, you know.

Jeremy   I had a meeting with Howard Jones today . . .

Susan   What, the eighties singer?

Jeremy   No, not that Howard Jones. Howard Jones Head of the Commission for –

Susan   Really? What did *he* want to meet you for?

Jeremy   Lovely guy, actually . . . He wanted to ask if I'd be interested in . . . running for Mayor.

She bursts out laughing.

Susan   What?

Jeremy   Don't laugh . . .

Susan   Oh my days, oh my days. That's fucking amazing.

Jeremy   Is it?

Susan   Are you crazy? What did you say? You said yes, right? Tell me you said yes.

Jeremy   I said I'd think about it.

Susan   What is there to think about? You'd make a brilliant Mayor.

Jeremy   What are you talking about, how do you know that?

Susan   You are a thoroughly decent, caring person. Isn't that what politics is about? We've always talked about how we could 'help' –

Jeremy   Yeah, running youth clubs, sporting days out!

Susan   Stop it . . .

Jeremy   It's not that. But . . .

Susan   There are no 'buts'. Oh, it's OK to run in harm's way when you see a kid about to get mugged but when opportunity to help many comes, you run from it?

Jeremy   I'm not running from it, I'm just . . .

Susan   I've been really uncomfortable with the way you've been feted for the whole shopping centre thing. The way they keep playing it round and round. I kept wondering why . . .

She picks up a book from the shelf. She reads from Ayi Kwei Armah's Two Thousand Seasons.

Susan   'How have we come to be mere mirrors to our annihilation? For whose entertainment shall we sing our agony? In what hopes?' *This* was the 'why'. You being asked to run is the why we had to endure the sight of a black man slapping a black child and it be celebrated. You just have to do it, Jeremy. End of story.

Jeremy   You think?

Susan   Yes, I do, I'll leave your arse if you don't.

Jeremy *stares at her, deep in thought.*

Lights.

Scene Four

Jennifer*'s den.* **Jennifer** *and* **Rav** *are playing Nintendo Wii tennis. We see their players on the projector – it is a live game.* **Jennifer** *scores a point just as the front-door buzzer goes off again. She runs to a wall and presses the open button, returns and serves.*

Jennifer   That all you got, bitch?! Take that!

Rav   Don't worry about me, I'm just warming up. But once the monster rises – like *that*, for instance . . .

He plays a great shot. But she returns it.

Jennifer (*laughing*)   Like what, Rav? Like what? What, my Right Honourable friend, did that do?

In dashes **Howard**.

Howard   Sorry I'm late, but I come bearing good news. We have our man. We have our Mayor!

Rav   What . . . what are you talking about?

Howard   Jeremy's gonna be here in about thirty minutes to meet you, so we should get right down to it.

Jennifer   Jeremy who?

Howard   Charles.

Jennifer   The guy from the TV show coming to my house?

Howard   Yes.

Jennifer   For why, for why, Howard?

Howard   Cause he's the one.

Rav   We agreed we were going to ask Jatpaul Singh. I've already asked him.

Howard (*all innocent*)   That's right, we did, didn't we? Oh!
What a pity.

Rav   It's not a pity. I've asked him and so that's that.

Howard *leans in, places his hands together and looks hugely sincere.*

Howard (*switching on the charm*)   Under normal circumstances
you know I would *absolutely* agree with you.

Rav   You already *did* agree with me, with us.

Howard (*carrying on*)   But I think this is an extraordinary
opportunity, I really do.

Rav   I know these moves, Howard, your sweet-voice number
doesn't work on me.

Howard (*returning to normal*)   As you know, I'd never heard
of Jeremy, but this is the one thing we cannot afford to get
wrong. I'm sure, Jennifer, you would agree.

Jennifer   Don't include me in your wrongdoings! We agreed
that Jatpaul was our man.

Howard   And I went home and I thought about it, took a
little counsel – and you know Jatpaul bores for Pakistan.

Rav *and* **Jennifer**   He's Indian.

Howard   Even bigger land mass to bore for.

Rav   I knew he'd do this, I just knew you'd do this.

Howard   Do what?

Rav   You weren't happy that he was Asian, were you?

Howard   What you talking about?

Rav   Jatpaul Singh is CEO of a five-hundred-million-pound
company. He's well respected. Has real and recognised
leadership talent . . .

Jennifer   Indeed he has.

Rav   But Howard doesn't want an Asian, he wants someone
who is black.

Howard   Not true.

Rav   It's true! I saw that look in your eye when we agreed I should approach him. I just knew you'd get up to something.

Howard   Rav, you and I have fought many battles together. I'm gonna ask you to take that back.

Rav   I'm not taking anything back. I'm upset, Howard.

Howard   This we can see.

Rav   Don't patronise me. We can't agree on one person and then wheel in someone else. It was already a done deal. It's unprofessional.

Howard   I wouldn't have done this if he was just someone else. This guy is special. And as great as he is, Jatpaul Singh just is not. He's a compromise. That's what you saw on my face.

Jennifer's *phone rings. She picks it up immediately.*

Jennifer   Oona, I'm gonna have to call you back girl. OK.

She shuts it off as the conversation continues. **Howard** *clocks that it was Oona King on the line.*

Howard (*'who's that'*)   Ms King?

Jennifer   Nose ache. Concentrate on what's happening here.

Rav   You know what, if we gonna be like this, let's be like this. I've seen your guy on telly – he's fine, but he's African Caribbean.

Jennifer *and* **Howard**   Which means?

Rav   You don't need me to tell you they come with a lot of extra baggage that I don't think this kind of adventure can handle.

Jennifer   Alright, Rav, I *was* on your side but you've just lost me!

Howard   Jeremy is clean as –

Rav You know that, do you?

Howard Yes, I do. My people checked him out. He has a second or third cousin that had some trouble with the law back in the day but who hasn't?

Rav Me.

Jennifer I haven't either.

Howard Well, whoopee for the both of you. Rav, Ravvv, let's not make this personal, brother. I apologise if this is going to put you in an embarrassing situation with Jatpaul and your peeps, but trust me on this, this guy is the one. His celebrity alone will take this out of the realms of colour and make him stand out. I just want you to meet him.

Rav For a post we've offered someone else already!

Howard (*flash of temper*) Look, if you wanna be a pussy about it I'll go and talk to Jatpaul, I'll apologise on bended knee . . .

Jennifer Howard!

Beat.

Howard (*switches to charm again*) Anyway, we could offer him Chief of Staff? Deputy Mayor, even. We all know that's where the power is.

Beat.

Rav We could do that, but as we all know that this is not about the winning but the running, you are taking the piss.

Howard I apologise . . . Now can I move this meeting just a little bit forward?

Rav You're going to anyway.

Howard (*playful*) Stop sulking, Rav, you bloody baby. Now, as you know, I can't be *seen* to be involved in this.

Rav Neither can I.

Howard If we go for Jeremy, Jennifer, your Campaign Black Vote are gonna have to create a separate unit and you front this all the way. I can get some set-up funding to it – but can you do that?

Jennifer   Do you think I should do my hair in twists or put the weave back in?

Howard   Pardon?

Jennifer   Don't ask me bloody stupid questions, of course we can handle this. I'd second myself and one other from the office.

Howard   Can the organisation run without you?

Jennifer   Ditto my previous answer. I've trained them well, Howard.

Howard   Good. So, now money? If we gonna do this right, we gonna need some of your Asian dosh Rav – you reckon you could siphon some of the avalanche that's flowing in to the Tory coffers right now and get some real tings for us?

Rav   That's all you ever want me for, isn't it, my Roladex?

Howard   Trust me, when you got one as big as yours . . .

Rav   Stop. I have to test the waters. It's a serious sell as to why it's one of you guys – that's the truth.

Howard   Just tell 'em after this it's gonna be Asian all the way, Prime Minister of colour – he's going to be Asian and you know that.

Rav   Alright. How much do you think we looking at to go independently?

Jennifer   Properly? Three to five mill. I *would* suggest we go via the parties. I've been badgering them to put someone of colour up for Mayor but they ain't buying it.

Howard   Who?

Jennifer (*slightly stutters*)   No one specific. Just someone of colour.

Howard   Male, female?

Jennifer   As I said, no one specifically.

Howard   Fine. Rav, gonna look to you to find one of those mills. Jennifer, we can easy raise a oner from the black church, can't we?

Jennifer   Yep, I have to say actually, as loath as I am from my marrow to agree with Howard . . . this is probably a more exciting prospect. You know, bucking the system, coming at it on our own terms.

Rav   Yeah. But that costs money, Jennifer. Howard, this Jeremy guy, does he stand for anything?

Howard   Don't swear at me! The last thing we need is someone who stands for something.

Rav   Are you sure you don't wanna think about Jatpaul? He don't stand for nothing but money.

Howard   I'm ignoring youuu! OK, assuming you like Jeremy as much as I do –

Jennifer (*lust in her eye*)   Oh, don't get it twisted, I already like him loads!

Howard   – the biggest challenge before us is to get white people to *trust* him.

Jennifer   But isn't the beauty of the forty-five per cent thing that we actually don't need them?

Howard   Come on.

Rav   I'm hearing, Howard; Londoners want to see black men dealing with the problems of their children. If he can do that – happy days.

He looks at his phone.

Howard   That's him. I'm gonna go downstairs and get him. I say again, if you don't like him, we'll find someone else, OK sulky? (*Into phone.*) Jeremy, I'll be there in a sec.

Jennifer *and* **Rav**   OK.

Howard *leaves the room. When it's clear he's gone:*

Jennifer   What's going on, Rav? When I first mentioned the idea of a black Mayor he was all *laissez-faire*, now he's all . . .

Rav (*avoiding*)   I don't know.

Jennifer   Don't be coy with me, you're his homeboy.

Rav   I'm always the last to know, Jennifer.

Jennifer   It can't be that he just wants to be king maker?

Rav   It could be, but I doubt it . . . I have heard some rumours of . . . I don't know, an internal investigation.

Jennifer   What for?

Rav   Seriously, I don't know. But he's losing a lot of friends, the current administration want their own boy. So maybe becoming the Mayor's daddy isn't too bad an option. Which is why he doesn't want Jatpul.

Jennifer   Thanks, Rav.

Rav   What for?

Jennifer   You could have walked just then but you didn't. This thing is only going to work with your wisdom in the driving seat. Oops, here they come. Show time.

Rav   Fuck it, I'm going to the toilet. I always like people to meet me for the first time when they're the ones sat down.

He ups and leaves just before **Howard** *and* **Jeremy** *walk into the room.*

Lights.

Scene Five

Jeremy*'s home.*

The door bell rings. **Alice** *– white, thirties – shouts from off.*

Alice   It's on the latch, come in and leave them on the doorstep, I'll be there in a second.

Enter **Lavelle**, *the boy from the shopping centre. He's still got a little bit of a shiner. He looks around. After a few beats* **Alice** *walks into the room. She screams.*

Alice   Ahhhh!

Lavelle *doesn't flinch.* **Jeremy** *comes running in.*

Jeremy   Alice –

He sees **Lavelle**.

Jeremy (*to* **Alice**)   Ah!

Lavelle   Did your girl think I was gonna jump her or something? She's the one that told me to come in, you know!

Alice   What's he doing here?

Jeremy (*cool but straight*)   Lavelle . . . This is my wife. She has a name and is standing right there. You could ask her yourself.

He doesn't look at her.

Lavelle   My question was actually rhetorical.

Alice   That's a big word for a . . .

Lavelle (*cool but challenging*)   What?

Alice (*trying to explain at first*)   I was expecting the Ocado delivery man. He just called to say . . . Why am I explaining myself? I don't expect to see my husband's attacker standing in the front room!

Lavelle   That's the great thing about life, innit, each day's a schoolday, as my grandad use to say.

Jeremy (*calm and cool, regarding* **Alice**)   Lavelle, can I ask you to have a little respect, please? You're in my home.

Lavelle   We can ask for what we like.

Jeremy (*asking her gently to leave*)   It's OK, darling. Sorry about that. We're good.

She fires daggers at both of them and leaves.

Lavelle   It's a bit dangerous leaving the door on the latch, innit?

Jeremy   Your probation officer said you'd be here at two. I was expecting you three hours ago.

Lavelle   Just when you think something isn't gonna happen, it just jumps up and kicks you in the arse – my grandad again. Well, he was Jamaican so he said 'ras'.

Jeremy   And you are Jamaican? British? What do you guys call yourselves now?

Lavelle (*ignores*)   Whatever. You got a big drum, innit?

Jeremy (*straight*)   What's a drum?

Lavelle   Gaff, house, yard!

Jeremy   Thank you.

Lavelle (*almost taking the piss out of his accent*)   My pleasure. Why'd you have us meet at your house anyway, took me ages to get here. Couldn't we have hooked up at the probation office or something?

Jeremy   I don't like those places. I wanted you to come to my home. The habitat you would have taken me away from had you successfully stabbed me.

They look at each other.

Lavelle   Can I just say if you're wanting, wishing, waiting for me to say sorry and all of that, it's not my tings, yeah. Far as I see you manned it, you box me in my face, we cool. But I don't need or want no mentor or any of that other stuff.

Jeremy   Then why are you here?

Lavelle   Cos you coerced me, innit? What's a mans to do? Go jailhouse or spend a few months with a some dry do-gooder? Not hard when they put it that way, is it?

Jeremy   You have a very interesting vocabulary, Lavelle. That kinda . . . I don't understand street black stuff and then, nice words . . .

Lavelle (*laughs*)   Nice words, what the hell are they?

Jeremy   Ones I might not expect from someone your age –

Lavelle   Like?

Jeremy   'Coerce'.

Lavelle   My mum never allowed to me speak of *black* in the negative. So she taught me other words. (*Deliberately.*) Innit?

Jeremy   May I ask that we ban the word 'innit' from all of our conversations? There are other ways to end sentences.

Lavelle   How many conversations we planning to have?

Jeremy   As many as we need?

Lavelle   Oh, is this the bit where you inform me that through the shared power of your intellect and reasoning you are going to penetrate parts of my psyche that no other has succeeded in reaching before and, in showing me the error of my ways with a new and sparkling clarity, I shall at once change my ways and never again, carry a knife, shall I?

Jeremy   That was the plan, yeah. I also planned to dress up in blackface and dance for you, in the hope of making you laugh, so you could see that I'm a great guy that can come down to your level and communicate . . .

Lavelle   What's blacking up your face got to do with me?

Jeremy   Cos you're a bit of a minstrel, aren't you, son?

Lavelle   I'm not your son!

Jeremy   You put on black warpaint on the street, play the nigger, so that we fear you but most of we all laugh at you. Yep, you're a little minstrel. But, actually, my job, what I really wanna do with you is not scrape off that mask but have you teach me how you wear it so well . . . I've read your school reports. Left with eleven A-stars and you didn't even bother to go to college? Let's forget bullshit and you teach me, school me, how you can live like that. Is that OK?

Lavelle *doesn't quite know what to say. At first.*

Lavelle   Is it true what I read in the *Metro*, you lost your job today?

Jeremy   No, I resigned. Sometimes a man has to accept the gifts placed before him.

Lavelle   Gifts?

Jeremy   The opportunity to sit back, relax, listen to an old soul record.

Lavelle   Now you talking my language, dog!

Jeremy   You think having permanent free time and a reasonably good career destroyed is 'your kind of language'?

Lavelle   That's what you get, *innit*, for punching children!

Jeremy   I thought we agreed we weren't going to use that word!

Lavelle   At the end of sentences. That, innit, my friend, was in the middle.

Jeremy   You have an answer for everything, don't you? Well, answer this. I see you as *my* gift, my gift to myself. Are you?

Lavelle   Alright, now you sounding like a weirdo. You know I ain't afraid to defend myself.

Jeremy   Defending yourself – is that what you call it, defending yourself?

Lavelle   You're getting very close to treading down that road stereotypical of chastisement.

Jeremy   No, no, no, I said you're my gift and not my pupil. I know all about the postcodes, I know all about having to walk the street as if you own it cos if you don't you'll be taken down. I know why you gripped up that boy in the shopping centre . . .

Lavelle (*jumps out*)   You don't know why I did that. So shut your mouth!

Jeremy   Pardon.

Lavelle   You heard me.

Lavelle *looks at him. He's not going to back down.*

Jeremy   You ever seen the movie *Trading Places* with Eddie Murphy and –

Lavelle   Yeah, yeah, yeah, that movie's hard.

Jeremy   I've always wanted to do that. An experiment that shows I could take a kid out of the ghetto, introduce him to the higher things and watch him grow before my very eyes.

Lavelle (*getting vex*)   I'm not your bloody experiment!

Jeremy (*laughs*)   OK, button one, the shopping centre, button two . . .

Lavelle   Stop fucking with me, Jeremy.

Jeremy   Don't swear with me.

Lavelle   You gotta to be kidding?

Jeremy   No, I ain't.

Lavelle   Don't you mean, no you're not?

Jeremy *smiles. Beat.*

Jeremy   I come from a generation that believes in reciprocity. Know what that means Lavelle?

Lavelle   Yes.

Jeremy   Even though you won't know how, you have helped me so much . . .

Lavelle   And what help do you think I need then, Winthorp?

Jeremy   Winthorp? Very good. You have watched the film. I don't know. You tell me what help you need?

Lavelle   I need help to, eh, get a drum like this – and a pretty wife like . . .

Jeremy   Alice.

Lavelle   Alice! Pretty white wife.

Jeremy   That's not what you need.

Lavelle (*poking*)   You're absolutely right. I don't check grey gal. My mum would never let me back in the house.

Jeremy (*ignores*)   I'll tell you what you need. See, I think you're already too deeply stained, corrupt beyond redemption. But even when we're as stained as you are, we can help stop the rot in others.

Lavelle   Well, that's a very flattering description. Thank you for that.

Jeremy   My pleasure. But that's what I think you need, you need to help others.

Lavelle   Is it? How do you know I'm not doing that already?

Jeremy   I don't. Like I said, school me.

Lavelle *doesn't speak for a bit, working out how to come back with an attack. But we can see he's a little fascinated by* **Jeremy**.

Lavelle   My mum said you look like the kinda black man that ain't been near anything black for a lifetime.

Jeremy   You speak a lot about your mum, don't you?

Lavelle   Is that what it is, you've forgotten what it's like, so you want me to show you? It's easy to forget when you living this large inn – sorry, isn't that so?

His mobile goes off.

Call me in five, I'm just finishing up.

Puts down the phone.

Jeremy   Do you know what I did before I was a . . . celebrity?

Lavelle   Does it matter? You're famous now and that's all there is to know. I got glock by a famous man, which makes me famous too.

Jeremy   You're famous because I hit you?

Lavelle   It don't matter what you do to get there, bruf, people stop me in the street and spud me.

Jeremy Why?

Lavelle I stood up to a big man.

Jeremy But you were on the floor bleeding.

Lavelle All mans fall, it's how you get up that counts. It was me or you. You got to me first. Respect due. Like I said, if it wasn't for you, I wouldn't be number one in the Youtube charts.

Jeremy And you're not disturbed by that?

Lavelle Nope.

Jeremy Not concerned that you're famous, as you call it, for waving a knife and being –

Lavelle Bruf, you're not hearing. I'm seventeen, you're a big man. The shame's all yours. Anyway, look, you done your good deed, I met my victim, can we just done this? I'll just tell my probo I'm here, sign whatever you gotta sign and we good. Ain't wasting your time, ain't wasting mine.

Jeremy And what is it you have to do at seventeen that an hour with me a week is such a drain on your schedule?

Lavelle To tell you the truth, I don't feel comfortable here. I ain't comfortable with you people.

Jeremy You people?

Lavelle Middle-class white folk.

Jeremy It may have passed your attention but –

Lavelle My mum told me that the only kinda black people that are successful are the wannabes. They may be black to most people, but to those that can really see those tainted ones, those stained beyond redemption . . . the mask is all apparent.

Jeremy Then we have something in common, don't we?

Lavelle Can we just call this quits, dude?

Jeremy 'Fraid not. (*Ironically.*) It seems I'm in need of lessons in blackness. So I'd like our one hour a week, please, to be dedicated to that endeavour. As you said, what's a mans to do? Go jailhouse or spend a few weeks with some dry do-gooder? It's kinda easy when you put it that way, isn't it? I'll see you on Wednesday. Don't be late.

Lavelle *kisses his teeth and leaves.*

After a few beats **Jeremy** *exhales. He's been playing and he's the one who's drained.*

Lights.

Scene Six

Jeremy's *home office.* **Howard** *is reading from a printout. He is speaking to* **Jeremy**, *who's off in the toilet. We hear the flush.*

Howard   The article is good, but . . .

Jeremy   No, no, then suggest away. I've never written one before, not for publication, so I really appreciate this.

Jeremy *runs in.* **Howard** *moves into smooth mode. A warm, helpful tone.*

Howard   Well, for me, your opening sentence could be a little clearer . . . middle less ambiguous maybe. But overall I suppose I just don't know what you're trying to say. Is it *society's* problem or *our* problem?

Jeremy   It think it's both.

Howard   You can't have both – too wishy-washy.

Jeremy   But it's what I feel.

Howard   I *think* what you're really saying is it's time to speak the truth: 'We have a problem and we need to deal with it.'

Jeremy *starts to type, then stops. We see his typing on the screen.*

Jeremy   Who's the 'we'?

Howard (*thinking*)   There it is. As 'black men' we have a problem and we have to deal with it. Write that down.

Jeremy   OK. Then I'd follow that right with my idea about –

Howard (*riffing*)   Oh no, no, I'd talk about your attack in the mall, then spell out how bad our children have become. List from the 'from-school-to-jail' stuff.

Jeremy   Really?

Howard   We can't hide from the truth. In fact, that's a better phrase – *that's* what you need to write down, scrub the other one.

Jeremy   Should a potential Mayor come down this hard on –

Howard   My brother, if you don't, you won't. My job, *our* job, is to make you acceptable to the general public. That's what you're interested in, aren't you – appealing to everyone?

Jeremy   Of course.

Howard (*nurturing*)   Well, the first thing a politician needs to exude is trust. They need to be able to trust you, trust *in* you. 'Can I trust him to say the things I want him to say? Trust him to be corrupt? Trust him to be truthful?' And that truth, my friend, starts with being honest about your own people. Come down hard on your own people, you automatically buy trust.

Jeremy   And what do they, your own community, think about it?

Howard   What, black people? Fuck black people, my friend. They do what the man tells them to do. In the old days massa would just line you up outside the big house, tell you what to think and off you'd go and think it. Now, they just put it in some glossy women's magazine, *EastEnders* or some tube throwaway and off you black masses go and do it. No, my friend, we got to get the white masses to trust you by any means necessary. The black man will follow.

Jeremy   I thought you said the thing about this is we don't need white people.

Howard (*snaps*) I never said that. That's the kind of shit Jennifer would say. Me, I know we will always need them. There's no place on earth right now that doesn't. Plus, she has great faith that she can get our people to the polls. *I* think *our* job is to empower *white* people to get to the polls and not be tribal.

Jeremy God, you're a lot more . . . cynical than I expected you to be. Every time I see you on the telly you're like –

Howard Smiling? And where did that get me? Stabbed in the back as soon as the new boys arrive. No. Today is another day my friend. We don't need to do that any more. You get this post, we definitely won't have to do that any more. Anyway, back to the article.

Jeremy Did I tell you that I asked the probation service if I could mentor Lavelle.

Howard Lavelle?

Jeremy The kid that attacked me?

Howard Why'd you do that?

Jeremy In fact, I am already mentoring him, he came over last week for the first time.

Howard To your house?

Jeremy I don't exactly have an office. Then we went out on Friday night. That's really where this article comes from.

Howard Listen, listen, listen, I now know why people love you, you are a man with a big heart. But never let those kind of people into your house, where you live. Are you crazy? Do you have security there?

Jeremy Of course I don't.

Howard What happens if you get robbed now, what happens to your wife?

Jeremy He's not going to rob me, for Christ's sake.

Howard Jeremy, we don't bleed, we *lead*, from the heart. First lesson.

Jeremy (*a little firm*) I'm not bleeding. If you must know, he's actually the reason I said yes to you. And not because he's a black kid, it's because – he's so bright, so bloody mixed up. They really *do* need someone other than Jah Rule or Fifty Cent.

Howard Yeah, yeah. But it's a bad idea, stop it. You get in, we set up schemes for kids like that. But never make it personal. Even more important now that you write this well. (*Starts to riff.*) Write, 'From cradle to jail, the children of the black underclass seem to be lacking the discipline other communities take for granted.'

Jeremy *types.*

Howard 'Until this fundamental problem is addressed our inner cities will continually be plagued with gun, knife and all other sorts of anti-social crimes we do not have the resource to defeat. And why must we always be blaming white society? Shouldn't we be raising our children better?'

Jeremy Didn't you say something like that the other day in your column?

Howard (*dismisses*) Yeah, yeah, more the merrier. Carrying on – 'Let us be hard on the source. Let us look at ways of fining parents' – no – 'teaching parents how to look after their children. Or maybe they just shouldn't be allowed to have them . . . ' No, can't say that. Let's stop at 'creating mechanisms for training parents'. Got all of that?

Jeremy I think so.

Howard (*remembers*) But you got to make it your own, right? This is *your* view, after all. Organic from you.

Jeremy OK

He starts to type.

Howard You're lucky – when I started out there was only Bernie, Diane and Paul in the house, and me and Trevor out here in the wild. No one else to help. I was the baby but all of us were fighting for a . . . huh! Now there's only Diane, and she doesn't talk to me. Actually Paul doesn't speak to me either. And when Bernie died, so did a little bit of me . . . You come at the right time, boy. Everything you need is right here. And if I ain't got it, Jennifer has. My girl has got juice.

Jeremy She seems nice.

Howard Nice? That girl's a terrier, mate. And every man I know has been trying to get a piece but she won't give it up! She likes you, though.

Jeremy (*playing it off*) As I said, I think she's nice. Didn't think Ravinder took to me very much, though.

Howard He's always like that, moody git, but he's a good man. Love him like cook food. So look, you get on and finish that article. I'll tidy up and tomorrow you meet with Jennifer and her team to brainstorm ideas that you're going to stand for.

Jeremy Normally I'm quite a confident man but I have to say I'm a little nervous about it all. I feel a little out of my depth.

Howard Ever ran for Mayor before?

Jeremy No.

Howard Then you're going to be.

Jeremy I'd feel a lot better if you were there at the meeting tomorrow?

Howard I can't be seen to be too involved in this, Jeremy. I'll call you before and after. Have faith, my brother. Life rewards the bold and we are being ferociously so.

He leaves. **Jeremy** *exhales.*

Jeremy Susan, what have you got me into?

He picks up his mobile and dials.

Lights.

Scene Seven

Jeremy's *front room.*

He and **Alice** *are on separate chairs, each reading. After a beat or so* **Jeremy** *puts down the book and rubs his eyes.*

Jeremy   God, this stuff is so dry.

Alice *doesn't respond.*

Jeremy (*reads from front cover*)   'Transcript of the Testimony given to REACH Parliamentary Select Committee on Black Youth and Crime 2007.' Wanna read?

Alice   No thanks.

Jeremy   Did you know that –

Alice   J, I'm reading.

Jeremy   Of course. Alright, I think that's it for me. Gonna hit it for the night . . . Night, love.

Alice   Night.

He stands to leave.

Jeremy   You OK, Alice? You've said about three words to me this evening.

Alice   I'm fine. Oh, your brother Mark called the landline. Said it seems you don't answer your mobile.

Jeremy   Oh yeah, yeah, I keep meaning to call him back. Oh, Angela's having a party on Saturday. She called after she read my article. She really liked it. Are you free?

Alice   I haven't read it yet. I'll read in the morning.

Jeremy   Fine. So we good for Angela's, right? She did ask specifically for you to come . . .

Alice (*laughs to herself*)   No, she didn't.

Jeremy   I just told you that she did. I'll show you the text if you want?

Alice   I don't wanna see your phone, J. And actually I'm busy on Saturday.

Jeremy   Doing what?

Alice   You go.

Jeremy   I don't want to go alone. I'm a bit bored of going places alone, Alice.

Alice   And I don't want to go to that party, alright? There's no need for us to have an argument about it.

Jeremy   Why not?

Alice   Because I don't like arguments.

Jeremy   Not argu – Why don't you want to go?

Alice   Jeremy, we've had this discussion before.

Jeremy   Is it something to do with Lavelle . . . ?

Alice   It doesn't have anything to do with anything. It can be anywhere where you and the 'in crowd' . . .

Jeremy   The what?

Alice (*snaps*)   I'm not going. Good night, Jeremy.

Jeremy (*disbelief*)   But you and Angela get on famously.

Alice (*exhausted*)   You always do what you wanna, so just go and parade as Mr Mayor-in-waiting.

Jeremy   Oh, so that's what it's about?!

Alice   Yes. It was hard enough being the wife of a reality TV 'star' – people pushing me out of the way to get your autograph, women slipping their numbers into your jacket . . .

Jeremy   No one's ever done that . . .

Alice   I saw, it, J. Just like I see all the fake kisses and hugs they give me and then go into the toilet, not knowing I'm there, mind you, and bitch me. 'How a fine man like Jeremy can be with one stick insect of a white woman . . . ' I've heard them, Jeremy.

Jeremy   When?

Alice   'He couldn't handle a black woman' – that's what I heard Marianne say . . . That's why I don't want to go to your parties.

Jeremy   Rubbish, she wouldn't have said that, those people are my . . .

Alice   Call them your friends, go on! People you've known since you've become famous, let me hear you call them your friends.

Jeremy   I just think . . . I just wish you'd stop bringing . . . things (*colour*) into areas that . . . You know, right now is the scariest period of my life and I'd really love it if you could find it in yourself to just support –

Alice   People *hate* politicians! I just don't understand why you would want to put yourself in that position, why you would want to put *me* in that position?

Jeremy   What do you want me to do, say no?

Alice   I don't want you to do anything, other than . . . well, actually . . . I want you to stop that boy coming to our house for one. Stop laughing like an idiot every time Howard calls, for two . . .

Jeremy   I do not.

Alice   You should hear yourself!

Jeremy   Listen, do you know how brilliant that man is? If I win this, it'll be because of him, his brain power, his intelligence.

Alice   God, you're sounding like one of them, and I'm not a politician's wife . . . (*Calms.*) When was the last time anyone around you looked at me as a person in my own right?

Jeremy   Have you had a bad day at work or something?

Alice   Don't be insulting.

Beat.

Alice (*hinting at his affair*)   Things others will get away with you will not, J. Things, *people*, that others can hide, your face gives away. They're gonna come after you, you're not the only one that's going to get hurt.

He thinks before he answers.

Jeremy   You know, all people care about these days, Alice, is that you're not corrupt, is that you're not stealing or being a hypocrite. I'm none of those things. I was born in a council estate and now I'm here, and tomorrow I could be . . .

Alice   But you're a liar. And liars get found out.

Jeremy   I don't know what you mean by that, but I'm going to go to bed . . . I'm sorry if you think I shouldn't do this. But how many times does something like this happen in a man's life? It's not like I have any children, I do this, I leave something behind.

The doorbell rings.

Who the hell is that?

He jumps up and heads to the door. **Lavelle** *enters.*

Jeremy   Lavelle, what kind of hour is this to turn up at my house?

Lavelle   What kind of shit is this, blud?

He hands **Jeremy** *a Daily Mail.*

Lavelle   My boys saw it on the internet. I had to run to the petrol station to get one for real. I just couldn't believe it . . . How can you write shit like this?

Jeremy   I didn't write –

Lavelle   You make me walk you around my ends, introduce you to people, my people and then you call us animals, living in pens, that need to be trained.

Jeremy   I didn't call anyone an animal. I was talking about the size of the homes the council pro – (*vides*)

Lavelle . . . What do you know about my mum, bruf? What do you know?

Jeremy Lavelle . . . I know you're upset, but calm down, it's 11.15 at night.

Alice Shall I call the police?

Jeremy No, don't do that. Go upstairs, Alice.

Lavelle Yeah call dem and tell 'em that your man here is a chief. And he's due to get dealt with. Don't you understand, when you talk about us like this time and time again, you turn us into shit. You lot do it all the time. I mean how am I suppose to feel, how we suppose to feel, J? You suppose to be a man, how you let the white man use you like his bitch!

Jeremy Don't you come here and start to abuse me! I'm sorry if you've been offended but –

Lavelle Fuck you and fuck your apology. Abuse? You ain't seen abuse yet. Trus dat. You're a punk and you're gonna pay!

He steams out. **Jeremy** *turns to* **Alice** *but can't quite look her in the eye.*

Scene Eight

Jennifer*'s den.* **Jennifer** *and* **Jeremy** *are talking.* **Jeremy** *is looking a little down.*

Jennifer . . . So the *Express* and the *Standard* want articles. Radio 4 want you on *Midweek*, which is great – love me some Radio 4. I've set you up – well, not directly, but I've suggested you speak at Diane Abbott's Black Schoolchildren Conference in a month to six weeks' time. Two thousand black women. You'll go down a storm, they'll love you.

Jeremy (*wary*) Is that one really necessary?

Jennifer Let me finish. I know you don't like the black thing exclusively, so I've got you an invitation for you for a keynote speech at the Jury Club. Focus there will be employment and business. Right down your avenue. Have you ever been unemployed?

Jeremy   Not really.

Jennifer   Not even for a little bit?

Jeremy   Well, a couple of weeks after uni maybe . . .

Jennifer   Good, then that's where you place the story. I know it stinks, but the stuff that really works, especially for black speakers, is if you could kinda tell a rags-to-responsibility kinda story – I once sold drugs now I attack the causes of anti-social behaviour blahdy blahdy. I can write something for you if you want.

Jeremy (*snaps*)   No!

Jennifer ('*are you sure*')   Some of the biggest names in business will be there, a good speech that night will place us just were we want you to be.

Jeremy   And that's where?

Jennifer   When we announce you're viewed by big business as a viable candidate.

Jeremy   When are we going to announce, as it were?

Jennifer   Oh, not for a good while yet. We gotta get what you stand for first.

Jeremy   And what do I stand for again?

Jennifer   I don't know, you tell me.

Jeremy   I thought that was your job, all of your jobs, to tell me what I think, what I stand for.

Jennifer's *phone goes of. She quickly picks it up while still staring at* **Jeremy**.

Jennifer   Ms Abbott, I'm gonna have to call you back . . . 'bout an hour.

Phone off. Having picked up something's not right.

Is everything OK, Jeremy?

Beat.

Jeremy   No, it's not. That article that went out, that everyone is now calling such a huge success, is, well, it's got my name on it but –

Jennifer   Oh please, there's a not a writer alive, bar probably Simon Jenkins that doesn't get edited and sub-edited to within a inch of his soul. That's the territory my friend, get used to it.

Jeremy   It wasn't the (*edit*) . . . Is this how it goes, Jennifer? You guys tell me what to say, I just say it? Cos I have to tell you, I'm no good at just taking orders. And that's how it feels right now.

Jennifer (*full charm mode*)   That's not how it's meant to be . . . Truly. If we are making you feel less than the . . . magnificent man that you are, then we are doing something terribly, terribly wrong – no, *I'm* doing something terribly wrong. I suggested you because I could see how brilliant you were, not just on the TV but in the shopping centre, in the shows you presented. Your integrity shone through. And if we are doing something that's messing with that . . . then we need to stop. Because without you we have nothing. You step back, then the whole black Mayor for 2012 is over. There's no one else. All we're trying to do is groom you for ultimate success. Groom you so that when those little black kids look up they don't see rubbish, but see *you*. You, Jeremy Charles.

Beat, as **Jeremy** *internally debates his frustration.*

Jeremy   Fine. Fine. I just needed to get it off my chest. This is all so new to me and . . .

Jennifer   No need to apologise. We have to talk to each other.

She moves behind him and starts to gently massage his shoulders.

It's a high-pressure game, Jeremy, the bad news is it's gonna get worse.

Jeremy   Wow, you're very good at this.

Jennifer   It's how I got through college.

Jeremy   You must have been living large. Ahhh!

Jennifer   Yep, a pressure knot right there . . . Did you do athletics? Cos your muscles are so well-defined.

Jeremy   Maybe you're working a little too hard.

She stops.

On my ego.

Jennifer   Sorry.

She carries on.

Jeremy   You're right about those kids, I was reading the REACH report the other night and one of the witnesses said something that no one seems to have picked up on.

Jennifer   Go ahead.

Jeremy   I don't know about you, but the biggest education I got when I first went to uni was seeing the kids from the big public schools and their absolute sense of entitlement. Our children just don't have that. We need to get them up to that speed, don't we?

Jennifer   And how do think we do that?

Jeremy   Have a six-day school week for chronically underachieving kids.

Jennifer   What? That's Westminster, Jeremy . . .

Jeremy (*'don't patronise me'*)   That I know, Jennifer. But are you telling me that the Mayor's office couldn't find a way to fund good old-fashioned Saturday schools, Jennifer? All we have to do is make it culturally compulsory. Asian and Jewish families do it.

Jennifer (*not convinced*)   What about the stigma of –

Jeremy   Stigma?! That's hoodoo-voodoo. What about the stigma of never having worked at fifty? Not being able to help

your children with their homework when they're twelve? Fuck
everything else, that's the only equality we need, Jennifer.
That's what I was trying to say in my article before Howard
butchered it. If I'm going to have to do this 'focus on our kids
thing', let me at least suggest something constructive, not just
moan and make them feel like crap. Don't laugh at me.

Jennifer   I wasn't laughing at you.

Beat.

Jeremy   Everyone's told me the Mayor's office is simply
there to advocate, then let's advocate something bigger than
just how to make the trains run quicker, or how to get cuter
parks. End of rant.

Jennifer *smiles.*

Jennifer   It was a good rant, though. A very good rant.

Jeremy   As was your massage . . .

She stares right at him.

Jennifer   Whenever you need another one, don't hesitate to
ask.

Jeremy   I won't . . .

They stare at each other, still in the zone.

Enter **Rav**. *He clocks the chemistry.*

Rav   Jennifer.

Jennifer   Hey, Rav? (*'What are you doing here?'*)

Rav   What the hell is wrong with your phone?

Jennifer   It ran out of juice. Sorry. What's up?

Rav   Go back to your office, Jennifer. I've just heard they are
going to go after Howard. Make sure all your funding shit
with him is clean . . .

Jennifer   Oh, we clean.

Rav   We all are. Till they start to make something up. Go
put your firewalls up.

Jennifer   Who've they got on him?

Rav   The boys who can make his shit come tumbling down. Ernst and Young.

Jennifer   Ooohh. And the Commission.

Rav   Who knows.

Jennifer   Thanks, Rav.

She hears him and leaves.

Jeremy   Rav, what does that mean for us? For this, if Howard goes down . . . ?

Rav (*making him state*)   What does it mean for you running for Mayor? Is that what you mean?

Jeremy   Yes, that's what I mean.

Rav   Well, we'll see, won't we?

Jeremy   You don't like me, do you?

Rav   Truth? No. I hate celebrity. The quicker we find an exit strategy the better. But, hey, who am I? Just the one that gets the money! Welcome to the world of black politics.

Lights.

Act Two

Scene One

Susan's *house*.

Susan *and* **Jeremy** *are dancing and singing along to a Michael Jackson CD.*

Susan *and* **Jeremy** (*singing*)
  'Get on the floor and dance with me,
  I love the way you shake your thing
  Especially . . . '

Susan *shakes down for* **Jeremy**.

Jeremy   'Get up, part down, shake your body down to the ground . . . '

Susan   'Part down – shake your body down to the ground'? What the hell are you talking about?

Jeremy   I don't know the words, and I'll put a tenner down that you don't either.

She slaps his hand.

Susan   Ten pound? You on. Wait a minute . . . wait a minute . . . it's coming . . .

She waits until the phrase comes back again and sings along.

  'Get up won't you g'on down,
  Shake your body won't you
  G'on get down.'

Ha! I want my money.

Jeremy   I was close!

Susan   You were nowhere near. Give me my money!

Jeremy   Ten pound for one word?

Susan (*monster voice*)   Give me my money or you gonna have to pay the hard way!

Jeremy   Is that so?

She runs at him and jumps on his back. False punches are flying as the song comes to an end.

Get off me, woman! Get off me! Don't make me have to get all bad on you . . .

He does a Michael Jackson leg move, then imitates MJ.

You wouldn't like me when I'm angry!

She manages to get him in a neck lock.

Alright, alright! I'll give you your money, woman.

She releases him. He gets out his wallet.

I've only got a fiver. Can I give you an IOU?

Susan   Only if it says I, Jeremy Charles, owe you, me, for ever and for ever.

Jeremy   Qualify 'for ever'?

Susan   This life, certainly dibs on the one after that.

Jeremy   And I get what from this everlasting binding?

Susan   Several lifetimes of me. What else could a man want?

She runs to the computer.

Susan   OK. Next track is . . .

Jeremy   Susan, we've been dancing for an hour. Could we sit down for a moment, please.

Susan   I haven't seen you in two weeks and you wanna start laying down the rules. No, tonight is boogie night. The next track will be . . .

Jeremy   I spoke to one of my advisers about you yesterday.

Susan *stops dead.*

Susan   OK, pause music.

Jeremy   I felt I had to, Suz. With all the pressure Howard's under, not that he tells me anything, but I just didn't want any . . . The public hate surprises.

Susan   You're sounding like a politician . . . What did he say?

Jeremy   Well, it wasn't what he said, actually, it was more what he didn't say.

Susan   So what didn't he say?

Jeremy   That it matters!

Susan   So why do I get the feeling that there's still something ominous hanging over my head?

Jeremy   I told him about us because I woke up this morning with a huge sense of dread. You ever have that? Not fear, but the feeling that something bad is going to happen.

Susan   Yep!

Jeremy   After I told him he simply asked what I intended to do.

Susan   And you said?

Jeremy   If I were to – maybe – leave my wife, when did he think was the best time to do that?

She looks at him.

Susan   Is that an option you're entertaining?

His mobile rings. It says 'Wife'.

She probably heard you. Don't you wanna answer that?

Jeremy   No.

He waits until it has rung off.

Susan   (*slightly agitated*)   And your adviser replied?

Jeremy   'The sooner the better' was his political view.

Susan   And his personal one?

Jeremy   He didn't feel equipped to have one of those, he said. Howard's such a great guy, you know, so clear, so straight.

Susan   So what are you going to do? And speak quickly, Jeremy.

*The phone rings again. This time **Jeremy** switches it to vibrate, but we can still hear it buzzing.*

Susan   Answer the flipping phone, Jeremy, or switch it off.

He waits for the buzzing to stop.

Jeremy   Do you remember my brother Mark?

Susan (*flips it at him*)   You don't let me meet your family, J. You've spoken about him lots. Yeah.

Jeremy   I went down to Peckham to see him today and I'm not talking about the posh end. He lives in a shit pad and looks crap. (*New idea.*) Don't you ever worry that you've had things so good that bad has just *got* to be on its way?

Susan   I never feel like that . . . No. The opposite maybe.

Jeremy   He and I were so close as kids, as young people, but he just wanted to hang around with the bad-boys and I hated the bad boy scene, and –

Susan   And what has this got to do with you leaving Alice, Jeremy?

Jeremy   Everything. Cos I'm slightly afraid if I do that the onset of this 'bad' will commence. I have no evidence for this, no logical explanation but for a gut feeling, like when I went for Lavelle in the shopping centre. Like when I came up and spoke to you in that restaurant. Mark stood by and watched as my parents poured all their money into me – private education, extra tuition – all because they said I was the one with 'brains' and he was the dunce one. I mean, if they hadn't done that who's to say that I wouldn't be the one living in the shit pad?

Susan   You're not the kind of man that –

Jeremy 'Kind of man'? There's no such thing. There's only luck, choices and the intersection where they collide. He could have held it against me, got in the way. But he accepted it as if his life was the sacrifice needed for me to –

His phone buzzes again.

Susan For Christ's sake answer the flipping phone!

He makes to leave the room.

You don't have to leave. I'm going to the toilet.

She walks off. He answers the phone.

Jeremy Hey, Alice, sorry I missed your . . . Calm down . . . calm down, Alice . . . I'm um, um, a few miles away . . . OK, I'm on my way . . . You've called the police, right? Do it now. I'll be twenty minutes . . . (*With urgency.*) Go wait in the car and lock the doors.

He locks off the phone and grabs for his jacket.

Susan! Susan!

She enters.

The house has been burgled; Alice thinks there's still someone in there . . . I –

She doesn't reply.

I'll come back and finish this?

He kisses her and dashes out of the house.

Scene Two

Lavelle's *house.*

Jeremy *is standing with* **Lavelle**'s *mother* **Sheila**, *thirty-twoish, head wrap covering locks. We can see from her attire she's a 'conscious', political woman.*

Sheila (*shouts*) Lavelle!

We hear him walking down the stairs. He enters and looks at **Jeremy** *blankly.*

Lavelle   What you doing here?

Jeremy   I want my stuff back.

Lavelle   What you talking about?

Jeremy   My house has been burgled and I know it was you. I want my things back, Lavelle.

Sheila   Hey, hold a funking minute . . .

Lavelle   Mum, it's alright. What's your house getting broke got to do with me?

Jeremy   Don't play games, Lavelle. TVs and iPods I don't give a toss about but there are personal things that I cannot –

Sheila   He said, what has this got to do with him?

Jeremy   He did it.

Sheila   Cos he's black he's got to have robbed your house?

Jeremy   Keep that bullshit for your social worker.

Lavelle   Can you have a little respect for my mother, please, or is it only in your house that rule applies?

Jeremy   I know it was you, you literally told me you were going to do it, you threatened me.

Lavelle   When?

Jeremy   At my own house, after the newspaper article.

Lavelle   I didn't threaten you.

Jeremy   My wife is sat at home crying, frightened in her own house because there is dog excrement in my living room.

Lavelle   You should train your beast better den innit!

Jeremy   We don't have a dog!

Sheila   Lower your voice in my house, please.

Jeremy   Wedding pictures and letters from my parents to my grandparents when they first arrived in England. Not to mention the jewellery. All of this may mean nothing to you, but they are everything to us and I simply want them back.

Lavelle   So have you told the police this?

Jeremy   I've told them about the robbery, yes.

Lavelle   That you think it's me?

Jeremy (*less confidently*)   I have given them a list of people that have been to my house of late.

Lavelle   Then they'll do their ting, and if there's something that says it's me, they'll come find me, right?

Jeremy   I don't care about them finding you Lavelle, no doubt you've done this a million times before and are very skilled at leaving no trace of yourself, but I care about my home being breached, being made insecure, I care about the trust that you have just broken.

Lavelle   Me? My mother taught me one thing. There are consequences to our actions, blud. You do good, the universe finds a way to pay you back; do bad, it hits you where it hurts you most, soon as it can . . . I lie, Mum?

Sheila   No son, you do not, that's how I raised you.

Lavelle   Me personally, and I could be wrong cos I don't know too much about that eastern stuff, but I'd say it was your bad karma hitting you back. Make people feel like shit, bruf, sometimes they'll act like it.

Jeremy   Do you not understand the harm you people do?

Sheila   'You people'?!

Jeremy   The harm you do to the few of us that are trying to do better for ourselves, better for all of us? (*He calms.*) You know what? Forget this. If this is about money I'm willing to pay.

Lavelle   Not that I know, but I got a feeling who ever broke into your drum didn't do it for money, J. Maybe now they feel evens. Maybe now they feel like equals.

Sheila   See, this is a conscious house, I taught my son that we should have very little tolerance for race traitors.

Jeremy   'Race traitors', what the hell are you talking about? Oh, but it's fine for him to be wielding knives in shopping centres – great upbringing that is.

Lavelle (*flips*)   Have you stopped to think that you have never once asked me why I was dealing that boy? Why I was willing to show him that we ain't no wastemans.

Jeremy   I didn't ask because –

Lavelle   – you're blinkered. Can't see beyond what you've been taught to see.

Jeremy (*almost childlike*)   OK, why were you attacking that kid, Lavelle?

Lavelle   Don't be stupid.

Jeremy   Is this how you let you son speak to grown men? In front of you he will–

Sheila   Why would I chastise him? If he saw a 'man' before him, he'd address a man . . . The boy he was 'roughing up' had thrown acid in a girl's face four doors down from here. No one would tell the police, though we all knew who it was. Lavelle and his crew were doing what men like you were suppose to, but don't have the balls to. Protect our community.

Jeremy   This is not the Wild Wild West – you go to the police –

Sheila   And that's why these boys hate you so much! A generation that have left the work of men to boys. And until you fix that, till you man up, you have no right to stand before my son accusing him of anything. Now, could you please, COME OUT ah me yard!

Jeremy *stares at them.*

Jeremy   I don't care what you say, I know it was you. I want my things back, Lavelle . . . And don't think you're getting out of coming to see me either. If you are three minutes late on

Wednesday, the *consequence* of that, the karmic return for that, will be, and I could be wrong cos I don't know too much about that prison stuff, but I believe they call it a holding cell in Feltham Young Offenders' Institute.

Lavelle   Ain't we done with dat yet − officially.

Jeremy   By my book we got three to go. See you Wednesday.

He exits. We hear the door slam.

Mother and son look at each other.

Lights.

Scene Three

Jennifer's *den.* .

Jennifer *and* **Jeremy** *are standing, speaking to* **Rav** *and* **Howard**. **Jeremy** *has just got to the end of a sort of presentation.*

Jeremy   . . . So what I think I'm saying is, I want to call this 'the new citizenship' . . . '*a* new citizenship' − either one. What do you think?

Jennifer   Well, I think it's great!

Howard   It's well thought through.

Jeremy (*excited*)   It's the politics of the common good. Changing the people of this city from being mere consumers to interconnected citizens that help each other. Do things for each other.

Rav (*probing for the answer*)   Telling people how to live, that's a difficult battle to fight in open ground.

Jeremy   I'm not telling people how to live, I'm suggesting a way of doing it better.

Howard (*sincere question*)   But who are you to do that?

Jeremy   A fellow Londoner! And isn't this what leadership is all about, Howard?

Howard   I hear you, and I would say this, wouldn't I, but I don't think you are at the point where you can sell that message in an article just yet.

Jeremy   I'm not selling it, I'm simply saying that this is my view.

Howard   But for people to accept this as a legitimate view to listen to, they need to know you better.

Jeremy   But won't an article like this *let them* know me better? If I put it on my Face page, Twitter it.

Howard *looks at* **Rav**.

Howard   Tell him, Rav.

Rav   The feedback I'm getting is, well, we need more of the stuff you wrote in the papers the other day. More self-analysis.

Jeremy   What does that mean?

Jennifer (*jumps in quickly*)   Forgive me speaking for you, Jeremy, but I think J is saying, feels, maybe to be taken seriously, he has to deliberately not go through the lens of –

Howard (*snaps in*)   That's a false binary. We're not saying he speaks about this for ever, we're saying let's get his trust numbers up the best way we can.

Jeremy   Hello, guys, I'm here. *I'm* saying, I have a certain perception of myself and talking about everything via this lens does not fit it. Anyone who knows me knows that I don't have an old-school agenda. I like to engage in ideas, new energies.

Howard   Public morality a new idea?

Jeremy   I'm not saying it's new, but it's a now idea. Binding people with a shared purpose, creating a revitalised youth. A revitalised notion of manh – of personhood even. It's what Barack is doing with Martin Luther King Day now being a community day.

Beat.

Howard   I'm with it but, listen, the few key people that I have spoken to like you, Jeremy. But they don't – know – you, sufficiently.

Rav   I agree. I am hitting barriers financially. People definitely need to know you a bit better. And I'm talking about young business people.

Jeremy   Which Jeremy you want them to know is what's concerning me. The one who speaks about everything through race, or the one who is diametrically opposed to that?

Howard *jumps up.*

Howard   They are not mutually exclusive, Jeremy, and like all good things the art lies in the cracks. So here's a crack. A friend of mine has just got a commission for Channel 5. The strand gets great numbers. High-end documentary looking at the hot topics of the day. She's agreed to have you present the programme. It's like ten steps up from the shit you used to do. She's taking a chance, but I persuaded her, you are the man. They start shooting in a few weeks, goes out a few weeks after that.

Jennifer (*becomes more interested*)   Sounds just what we need.

Howard   Of course it's just what we need.

Jeremy   What's it about?

Beat.

Howard   There's been an explosion of rapes in the inner city of young girls. It seems the principal culprits are young black men.

Jeremy (*cool*)   I'm not doing that, Howard.

Howard   What do you mean, you're not doing that?

Jeremy   Exactly what I said. I'm not doing that.

Howard   I've already told her you would.

Jeremy   And I've just told you I don't want to continually be bound by . . . You do realise that there are consequences of continually telling these children that they are –

Howard   And I've already told you that there'll be a time when you will not be *allowed* to talk about race, but until that point, this is our strategy and it's a successful one.

Jeremy   Aren't we simply bored about talking about young black boys?

Howard   It would seem not.

Jeremy   I never hear them racialise paedophilia, or serial killers. (*Does voice.*) 'Hi, this is *Despatches*, and I want to look at why serial killers in this country are exclusively white!' I'm not doing it.

Howard   Are you spending too much time with Lavelly or whatever his name is? Because last time I looked, you were slapping black boys in the face for less than this and smiling about it . . .

Jeremy   I told you before, I was not smiling and I was –

Howard   This is why I told you not to let that boy in your house. He's got you running scared.

Jeremy (*almost surrenders*)   So what if he has? It's not just him. My cousin called me from St Albans – he never calls me. My brother called. He called to ask 'why would I write such a thing?' Don't I know that he has boy children? I mean, God, could you stand up to such scrutiny? Daily negative exposure?

Howard   I have for twenty years. What do *you* think I'm going through now?

Jeremy   Well, bully for you, but I know when *I* was young, I wouldn't be able to handle this . . .

Howard (*snaps*)   Well, maybe you just weren't strong enough! Maybe they need this to toughen, to change, to straighten them up.

Jennifer (*tries to calm*)   Howard, maybe we should – (*chill.*)

Howard   No. This documentary is a great opportunity, Jennifer. There'll be live debates on all the radio stations after this, there'll be a hundred article requests. Rape captures the attention of people, believe! This is how we make him. Do this well and maybe we don't have to do this stuff any more. But for now, you alone, my friend, celebrity or not, are not pulling in the money or support we need to make this thing happen. I've gone out of my way to get you in the frame and I'm fucked if I'm gonna just bow to you being over-sensitive about the feeling of those bloody little hooligans.

Rav   Howard!

Jeremy   This is why they hate us for this very thing – we'll expose them, but do nothing to protect them?

Howard (*to* **Jennifer**)   This is not the Jeremy I met the other month.

Jeremy   Well, this is the Jeremy you have now, and I don't want to do it, Howard. All my life I have stayed clear of race and now you want me to dive head on into a pit filled with shit time and time again.

Howard   Get it right, it's filled with roses on the other side, my friend.

Jeremy   I don't care. I'm not doing it.

Rav *tries another angle.*

Rav   How many times a week, say, do you think about the disabled?

Jeremy   What? I don't know.

Rav   I'd wager you only think about then when there's a disabled person in front of you. How many conversations do you think you have with said disabled person where the text or subtext isn't about disability?

Jeremy   What has this got to do with anything?

Rav   My friend, it is not until you really really know someone that you look past their disability and begin to have real conversations. This isn't about black and white, it's about access and exposure. And the overwhelming majority of white people have limited exposure to black people on equal terms.

Howard   And I'm giving you that opportunity.

Jeremy   And I'm not taking it.

Howard *switches again.*

Howard   Then I don't know about you guys, but I think you've lost your nerve. Your house being robbed and stuff, I think you should step back and see if this really is something you still wanna do. Cos I don't tolerate weakness around me. You don't survive in this business by being weak, sensitive or naive and you are displaying all three right now. Those kids will stab you in you chest before you fucking know it and you wanna throw away a chance of a lifetime for them? Then do that, Jeremy. Throw it away. In fact, fuck off now and think about it, because I for one think you're a bottler. And there's no place in this world for bottlers. Certainly not mine.

Silence. **Jeremy** *walks out. We hear the door slam.*

Jennifer   Howard, I know you're under pressure right now, but there's no need to go off on him like that!

Howard   And because you fancy him . . .

Jennifer   Stop! Don't turn on me!

Howard   He's showing weakness, Jennifer; it's too soon. Let's drop him.

Rav   Want me to call Jatpaul? He's still there.

Jennifer   He stood up to you, how many people do that?

Her phone rings. She picks up.

Howard   Too many at present! Plus, I've been hearing rumours about his love life.

Jennifer   Ms D Butler, I'm *definitely* gonna have to call you back. (*Intently interested.*) What rumours?

Rav   If you don't wanna go for Jatpaul, then maybe we should cut the boy some slack and let him feel that he's at least contributing to this thing.

Howard   But he doesn't know what he's doing, Ravinder.
I hate people that don't listen to advice that's in their best
interest.

Rav   Then listen to me. Whether Jeremy runs then falls and
someone *else* has to take the baton from there, we need the
general public to grasp the the demographical facts. Jeremy is
the perfect guy to bring that message to them. Right now,
there's no one better. Not you, not anyone.

Jennifer (*offended*)   We can't just use the man as a stalking
horse, Rav.

Howard   That's what you're doing.

Jennifer   I beg your pardon?

Howard   Don't think I can't see through your little girly
plans. It's clever and I like it, but I can see youuuuu!

Jennifer   What are you talking about?

Howard   You designed this whole exercise to put pressure
on the party to select your mate Oona.

Jennifer   That is not true! . . . And even if it were, it
certainly isn't now. This man can do it, his ideas, his passion.
He can do this.

Rav (*jumps in*)   Howard, I'm gonna call my man unless you
call, apologise and give Jeremy some latitude. Are you hearing
me?

Beat.

Howard   Alright. I'm hearing you. I'll call and apologise.

Jennifer   You need to do more than that. We need to give
him the reins to say what he wants to say.

Howard   Alright, alright. Jennifer, let him speak about his
'citizen shit' at Diane's school conference thingy. But he's
doing that bloody doc, if it's the death of me, deal?!

Jennifer   Deal.

Howard   You sit on his every word, though.

They nod and **Howard** *walks off.*

Jennifer   He's such a wanker!

He walks back.

Howard   Fucking heard that.

Lights.

Scene Four

Jeremy*'s home office.*

Jennifer *is standing alone, on the phone to* **Howard**.

Jennifer   . . . Really? Are you sure? . . . Fine but, Howard, what's happened? . . . Has he really? Which paper does he work for now? . . . OK, you run. I'll call you as soon as I've left.

She cuts the call and continues to read the speech in her hand.

Enter **Jeremy** *who overheard a bit of the conversation. He stands staring at her as she reads, almost wanting her to say something contrary.*

Jeremy   So?

Jennifer   It's good . . . very good.

Jeremy   Really?

Jennifer   Yeah. I mean it's a little –

Jeremy (*jumps in hard*)   What?

Jennifer   Long. But, no, the only thing I would add is . . . I think you should say that you intend to run for Mayor.

Beat.

Jeremy   I thought we weren't going to announce that until –

Jennifer   I know, but the boys think the quicker we get you out there, the broader the discussion becomes. Start building momentum.

Jeremy *punches the air.* **Jennifer** *doesn't look so pleased.*

Jeremy   Brilliant. Yes! It wasn't the boys, *you* did that, didn't you? You persuaded them, didn't you?

Jennifer   I think it was your outburst the other day that persuaded them.

Without side, he runs up and kisses her on the forehead.

Jeremy   Thank you. Thank you. I was gonna jack this whole shit in today if you didn't like what I wrote. Thank you.

Beat.

Jennifer (*as subtly as she can*)   Jeremy, are you sure this is something you want?

Jennifer   Of course, why would you say that?

Howard   Just, once we announce, there's no stepping back. You're in it.

Jeremy   To win it. I got to believe that Jennifer . . . Do you not?

Jennifer (*not entirely convincing*)   No, I believe . . . I just wanna make sure that you do.

Jeremy   Well, I do.

Jennifer   Good. Well, OK, I think this is the perfect audience to announce to. Two thousand screaming black mothers! We gonna have a ball.

The front bell rings.

Jeremy   Excuse me.

Jeremy *goes off to open the door.*

Jeremy (*off*)   Lavelle? It's Tuesday?

Lavelle (*almost humbled*)   This ain't no long tings.

Jeremy   No, no, come in, I'm in the middle of a meeting but it's . . .

They enter the room.

Jeremy   Jennifer, this is –

Jennifer   I know. Hi, Lavelle.

Lavelle   What's up?

Jennifer   I'm very well, thank you.

Lavelle *looks a little agitated.*

Lavelle   Listen, if you on a big one, I can . . .

Jeremy (*looks to* **Jennifer**)   No, no, no. We were just about to take a break, weren't we?

Jennifer   Yep, I'm gonna have a fag in the garden.

Jeremy   Fine.

She leaves. The boys sit down. **Lavelle** *looks at* **Jennifer** *as she exits.*

Lavelle   Alice not here, I take it?

Jeremy   No, it's nothing like that. Alice is at her mother's. Look, I wanted to apologise for the other day. I shouldn't have assumed that it was you, I was just –

While he's speaking **Lavelle** *opens his backpack and takes out some jewellery, letters, two iPods etc.* **Jeremy** *looks on.*

Lavelle   Some of the other stuff I might be able to get hold of later, but it's gonna take a little work.

Jeremy *doesn't speak.*

Lavelle   I didn't have to broke your house, Jeremy. Just knew if I told the right boys where you lived, sooner or later . . .

Beat as **Jeremy** *stands and walks away.*

Lavelle   The important thing though is that I got 'em back, right?

Jeremy   And I'm supposed to say thank you for that?

Lavelle   It's what you asked for? . . . And I was just
wondering, seeing as I *did* get some of your things back, if you
could . . . Look, I'm use to sorting stuff out myself, yeah, but
this is a little . . . I just wonder if you might be able to . . .

Jeremy (*stares at him*)   Are you in trouble?

Lavelle *takes out a photo and hands it to* **Jeremy**.

Lavelle   My uncle is. This is him.

He reads the back.

Jeremy   Why's it got written on the back, 'Love you, son'?

Lavelle   He calls me son because I asked him to.

Jeremy   OK. And I can help you how?

Lavelle   My uncle's a street journalist. He's crazy, does shit
he shouldn't do, goes places he shouldn't go . . . My mother's
always scared and cussing him. If he gets into trouble in
foreign, what can we do? On Monday we heard from a friend
that he was on a ship delivering toys and dat to Gaza. It got
raided by the Israeli army and they arrested everyone on it.
They say he's in some high security prison that no one's got
access to.

Jeremy   I've not seen anything on the news about that.

Lavelle   Exactly! There were a few bits on the internet, but
now nothing. Look, I've printed all I could find . . .

He takes some printouts from his bag. **Jeremy** *scans them.*

Lavelle   That's his name on the top there, Tony Grant. We
can't find anything anywhere. My mum wants to print out
flyers and hand them out on the street and outside Parliament,
but I know that's not how you do things any more, is it? I
mean, I'm not criticising my mum but . . .

Jeremy   I know. And how do you think I can help?

Lavelle   You're famous, J. You're a celebrity. You could talk
about it on the news, innit, write an article like you did the
other day, people will listen to you and maybe then we'll hear

something. They'll be forced to tell us something! You can help spread the word.

Jeremy   . . . Lavelle.

Lavelle (*spits it out*)   My mum and I don't know how to do this. You're the only person I can turn to.

Jeremy   Even if all of this was true . . . I can't just pick the phone and call ITN?

Lavelle   Of course you can. You're Jeremy Charles from the TV!

Jeremy   The real world doesn't work like that, Lavelle.

Lavelle   Yes, it does. I hear celebrities talking about everything all the time. I read about it every day. J, all I'm asking is that you put it in your Twitter – 'Where is Tony Grant? Why's he being held?' Knock it on your Facebook. I mean you've got six thousand friends on your page. Call some of the powerful people you know.

Jeremy   I don't have that kinda juice.

Lavelle   Why are you looking so scared, blud? You wanted your tings back, you came to me. I want news on my uncle, I come to you. What's the point of being on TV all the time when, when you need them, you ain't got no juice? What's the point of being on the inside if you can't do anything that counts? Hasn't that been your argument to me all along – nothing changes from the outside?

This stings **Jeremy**.

Jeremy   Wait. Let me speak to Jennifer.

Jeremy *leaves the room with papers. After a few beats he returns with* **Jennifer**.

Jennifer   I've seen an email about this. That's your uncle?

Lavelle   Yeah.

Jennifer   It says here that they've already got legal representation.

Lavelle   But Thomas, his mate, said to Mum that they are not letting them see their lawyers.

He takes a printout of another email and hands it to her.

Jennifer   You're a very together young man.

Lavelle   Why isn't it on the news? That's what's killing me, a man get mugged round the corner it's on a fifteen-minute loop, man gets kidnapped and . . .

Jennifer   It's a lot more complicated than that. I mean, you're right, this is outrageous. But at this moment in time I don't think this is something that Jeremy can get himself involved in. I can go –

Lavelle   Why the hell not?

Jeremy (*gently*)   Yeah?

Jennifer (*almost sighs, almost apologises*)   Brother, we just don't do Israel. It's too complicated, too –

Jeremy   God, you sound just like Howard . . .

Jennifer   That's unfair.

Jeremy   Why can't we mention it at the conference, say? There'll be hundreds of press there.

Lavelle   That's what I'm talking about . . .

Jennifer (*a little firmer*)   Can we have this conversation – (*another time.*)

Lavelle's *mobile goes off.*

Lavelle   Yo! I'm coming! (*Turns to* **Jennifer** *and* **Jeremy**.)

'We must fight so that when we meet our end,
It may be said that we tackled whatever we could,
That battle-fit we lived, and though defeated,
Not without glory fought.'

Henry Reed's 'Unarmed Combat'. My uncle's favorite poem. I'm not asking Jeremy to run in there and pull him out, Jennifer. Just that he asks a question. I gotta go.

He leaves. **Jeremy** *looks to* **Jennifer**.

Jennifer   Don't look at me like that, Jeremy. This is not something to be trifled with.

Jeremy   It's the boy's uncle.

Jennifer   We don't know that, we don't know anything.

Jeremy   I'm not talking about making pronouncements, but if these people have been wrongly arrested and imprisoned –

Jennifer   You've just made one right there, Jeremy. Experienced, brilliant politicians avoid this subject like the plague.

Jeremy   I'm not a politician.

Jennifer   And you never will be if you don't learn to listen!

Jeremy   This boy has just crossed a threshold, Jennifer. He's acknowledged that the street has no real power. Isn't it my duty to help him, isn't *our* duty to confirm this as fact?

Jennifer   It's your duty to look after yourself! Jeremy, there are things going on above your head that you have no understanding of. I am trying to protect you from them – trying to make this a real prospect.

Jeremy   What don't I understand, Jennifer? That I'm being set up? That once the grand political point has been made with celebrity branding I'm disposable? That Howard really fancies it himself but is so hated by everyone that he'll wait on the inside, ready to pounce when I fall? Do you honestly think I'm that *stupid* to not have seen that from the get-go? But I also believe in whatever fucked-up way it manifests, in the possibility, the minute possibility of . . . that I was meant to be here, be on this road at this time . . . (*Changes gear.*) I have a lover, Jennifer, in the real sense of the word in that she *loves* me. *She* wants me to do this gig because if ever I'm to leave my wife, *now* is the time. I have a wife that *doesn't* want me to do this gig, because *she* knows that the moment I do this, our lack of love will be exposed to the world. And I have you, Jennifer – who I believe actually wants me to do this because you believe I can. Why then would you play by old rules when we both know that this day is about the creation of new ones?!

Jennifer   Because the new rules have not been printed.

Jeremy   Jennifer, you are a forty-something-year-old black woman. According to the rules you should be a supervisor in Sainsbury's but you're not. You're the head of a brilliant and dynamic organisation. According to the rules, I, like most of my peers should have been in prison or at least borstal . . . All of these rules, rules about what white people will accept of us, about what is and isn't black, they belong to the twentieth century –

Jennifer   But Jeremy, this is Israel.

Jeremy   I don't care, I'm bored of it all. I don't really give a monkey's about the Middle East, Jennifer. But this isn't about me, this is about Lavelle and showing that boy that being on the inside is worth something. All want to do is put a sentence or two at the end of my speech tomorrow. That is all, for Christ sake. Let me do that.

Jennifer   If you weren't running for Mayor you could do what you want, but –

Jeremy (*calm*)   If I wasn't running for Mayor I wouldn't be making the speech!

Jennifer   Howard would go –

Jeremy   Fuck Howard!

Jennifer (*calming*)   J, if this is all true, Jon Snow will be on it in a heartbeat.

Jeremy   But Lavelle didn't ask Jon Snow, did he? He asked me . . .

She thinks.

Lights.

Scene Five

Jeremy *walks into his house.* **Alice** *is in the front room with a small bag. The atmosphere is tense.*

Jeremy   Hey, Alice. Good to see you.

Alice   I just popped back to get some more clothes . . .

Jeremy   How is Mum?

Alice   Fine.

Silence.

I see in today's papers that your boy Howard's in a bit of hot water?

Jeremy   What?

Alice   They've called the police in on him.

Jeremy   What?

Alice   Have we heard from the police yet, Jeremy?

He clocks that she is standing right by the returned jewellery. He continues to text.

Jeremy   Yes, sorry, I meant to call you yesterday. They found a few of our items in a bin on the High Street and some others in a –

Alice   Robbers are getting choosy these days. Binning 80-gig iPods?

Jeremy   Just one minute . . .

He finishes texting.

Alice   Where have you been staying, Jeremy?

This re-focuses **Jeremy**'s *mind. He puts down the phone.*

Jeremy   How do you mean?

Alice   Since I've been at my mother's. Where have you been staying? The bed looks hardly slept in.

Jeremy   I haven't got time for this. I'm supposed to be announcing tonight –

Alice   Who brought this back in our house. Was it that boy?

Jeremy   Yes, it was.

Alice   Good, so you've informed the police and they're arresting him, are they?

Jeremy   I don't see the point in further criminalising the boy, Alice . . .

Alice   'Further criminalise'? The boy is a criminal. He broke into our house. You said if it was him you'd bring down the full weight of the law . . . you promised.

Jeremy   It's not that simple, Alice.

Alice   Yes, it is. 999.

Jeremy   Alice, this kid has been sent into my life to –

Alice   – excrete in our living room.

Jeremy   – to make me . . . look at things – (*differently.*)

Alice   You'd be a shit Mayor. All you do is make excuses.

Jeremy   I'm not making excuses, I'm trying to protect this kid. We are supposed to stick our necks out for people sometimes, Alice . . .

Alice   What . . . ?

Jeremy   That's what we're here for. I didn't grow up on the sunny side of Wimbledon, Alice. Where I lived we only survived because people looked out us, people protected me.

Alice   And who's protecting me, Jeremy? While you're out for saving the scum of the earth, who's protecting me? What am I supposed to do?

Jeremy   Stand by me!

Alice (*calm*)   And if I can't?

He doesn't answer at first. Then changes.

Jeremy   Then we should stop.

Beat.

If I've learnt one thing of late it is that I hate being caged. We went through so much to be together that we have prefered to live empty lives. We don't love each other, Alice. We haven't for years. You're right, I didn't sleep here last night. I slept at Susan's.

Alice   At last you've paid me the decency of being honest. But don't you ever speak to me . . .

Jeremy   You want to move back here, and I'll –

Alice   No. But I don't want you to live here either.

Jeremy   Then let's sell.

Alice   It's a crap time.

Jeremy   Then let's rent it out and split it till we can.

Alice   Fine. Angela and her girls will be well pleased. You've finally left me for a sister.

Jeremy *ignores. Beat.*

Alice   None of those people around you care, Jeremy. None of them . . . Be careful with your new-found freedom.

She picks up jewellery.

Alice   May you have all you wish for.

Jeremy   The Chinese call that a curse.

Alice   Yes, they do!

Lights. In the darkness we hear the voice of Diane Abbott.

Dianne Abbot (*voice*)   And it gives me great pleasure to introduce to you our penultimate speaker, educationalist and writer Kenneth James.

We hear the thousand-deep audience applaud.

Scene Six

*Backstage, Black Children in Education conference. Green room/dressing
room.* **Jeremy** *is sitting reading through his speech.* **Howard** *walks in
looking a little ruffled.*

Howard   There you are.

Jeremy   Howard, where have you been? I've been trying to
call you all –

Howard   I know, I know, I had to switch my phone off. It's
been crazy. I take it you've heard?

Jeremy   Bits and pieces. But I couldn't get hold of anyone
to check?

Howard   Because they're all firefighting . . . Remember
what they did to Lee Jasper? Even those remotely associated
with him got hung, drawn and quartered. No, my friend, it's
all hands to the deck.

Jeremy   What did you do? They say you did –

Howard   Do you know how many years of my life I have
given to public service? Do you know how much of my soul I
have given to them just so that they could, I could . . . and
then come after me for this one tiny thing? I allow payments
to go through to a few organisations that *they* have already
said we are going to fund, just hadn't rubber-stamped –
organisations that would have gone down if they didn't get
the money pronto, and they wanna get me for that? Well, as
NWA said, they've chosen the wrong nigger to fuck wid!
Enough! Listen, you're gonna be here on your own tonight,
I'm sorry about that, but probably in the long run it's a good
thing. Jennifer's given me the heads-up on your speech.

Jeremy   How much of a heads-up?

Howard   Israel heads-up. I don't give a toss. Say what the
hell you want. Any other trouble spot you wanna talk about?
Iran? China? Go ahead. But I do need you to . . . Well, well,
I do need you to do something for me. I need you to go out
there and big me up . . .

Jeremy   Big you up?

Howard   Yeah, say nice things about me. Well, actually, more than nice, I need you to be damnright celebratory. Unless we head this thing off, tomorrow's papers are going to be dominated by me and my so-called misdemeanours. I mean, the fucking white boys do this all the time, but that's another subject. You announcing that you gonna run for Mayor couldn't have happened at a better time. The London papers have to go with that. When they report you, they'll report on what you said. So all you need to say is, I don't know, that I was your role-model from afar, showed you that it was all possible, talk about the things I've done for this country, for the black community specifically – that's really important. What taking someone like me down would mean to the black community. We got to play that card and we've got to play it hard . . .

Jeremy   But you always say fuck the black community?

Howard   No, I don't! And even if I said something that sounded like that, I meant . . . we can't be bound by, mustn't be bound by . . . But anyway, I've written a few notes for you.

Jeremy   You knew this was going to happen? That news of your investigation was going to be in the press today . . . ?

Howard   Of course I didn't.

Jeremy   That's why you moved announcing my candidacy forward?

Howard   What are you talking about? Can we forget this and get back to the here and now? . . . It's important not to make it too long but to say, like Barack, I was the first president of my student . . .

Jeremy   I don't understand why you're asking me to do this.

Howard   Because if I don't get the support of those black people out there in the audience, I am fucked. If we don't mobilise those people around supporting their leaders in times of crisis we will for ever have our leaders chosen for us, every time. Have I articulated that in a way that allows you to understand that your job is to stand by me?

Jeremy   But then I go down with you as well?

Howard   I'm not going anywhere, my friend.

Jeremy   You're asking me to throw away my one chance to really do something usef – ?

Howard   My friend, let's be clear, without me there is no 'doing something'. There is no you. You want to run for Mayor, you wanna help the bla-blars and the et cetera et ceteras? Well, your help starts here. Read what I've written and go out there and sell my virtues, Jeremy.

Jeremy   Did you do it?

Howard   What?

Jeremy   What they are accusing you of?

Howard   I've already told you, I did what anybody else would have done. Half the reason they delayed their funding was to take away my power base, and I was not going to have that. No way. Now, go out there and announce yourself as the representation of the tipping point – the time black Londoners got their voice, got some power, and understood how to use it.

*An **Assistant** enters the room.*

Assistant   Mr Charles, could you come with me, please? You're on in a second. I need to take you to the stage directly.

Jeremy   Of course.

Howard   Do the right thing, brother. Remember, save me, save yourself.

Assistant   Mr Charles . . .

Jeremy *leaves.*

*As the lights go down we hear **Dianne Abbott**'s announcement.*

Dianne Abbot (*voice*)   And so it gives me great pleasure to introduce the star of the evening, the one and only – and ladies, calm down now – but big up Jeremy Charlesssss.

We hear the applause.

Jeremy (*off*)   Thank you, thank you.

Slow lights.

Scene Seven

Park.

Jeremy *and* **Susan** *are walking together. She is reading to him. Eventually they sit on a bench.*

Susan   'A people deaf to purpose are lost . . . bodies, mere corpses, awaiting final burial . . . '

Jeremy   A happy read, this book, then!

Susan   Be quiet – I love this bit. 'But it is your nature *spring* to give, to revive. Giving, receiving, receiving, giving . . . it is that, which continues life . . . and it is you that I see coming towards me in the distance. I know I will survive this drought because you, spring, will soon be here.'

Jeremy   Ever the optimist, aren't you?

Susan   No. I can just see it, that's all. I can see it in you, in how you handled last night, in how the world feels this morning. Because of you I tracked down that tenant, you know?

Jeremy   Which one?

Susan   The guy that lost all of his worldly possessions when we burned his –

Jeremy   Oh yeah. He OK?

Susan   No, but he was so pleased to see me. He smiled so hard and just said, 'You know this is black people time?!' And couldn't stop laughing.

Susan *spots* **Lavelle**.

Susan   Oh, here we go. I'll meet you at the café at the top end?

Jeremy   Oh, here we go. I'm gonna give you a . . .

He kisses her and she leaves. **Lavelle** *comes running up.*

Lavelle   Who's dat? Dat ain't your missus!

Jeremy   Long story. You're late!

Lavelle   And what you got me coming all the way here for? I ain't seen a single black man in this park, apart from you. I don't feel safe blud.

They start to walk.

Jeremy   Hampstead Heath is one of the most –

Lavelle   I don't care what it is, I got hay fever, J, can we not go to a park at my ends or something?

Jeremy   This is your ends, Lavelle. Look over there, well, you can't quite see it all, but in the seventeenth century a young black girl lived in that huge house. Had an allowance, servants. But as soon as she stepped out every one would look down on her, associate her with what the lowest of the low.

Lavelle   She should have just stayed in her yard then?

Jeremy   Why should she have to do that, Lavelle? Do you know what that pressure does to you? Do you know what the cost of wearing that mask does to you?

Lavelle   I'd say I do.

Jeremy   Yesterday I went onto a stage, hall was filled with two thousand black people. Lavelle, up until the other day when I saw more than three black people together I crossed the street. But I stood in front of those people and there were two roads before me. The wrong road and the wrong road. And you know what I did? I thought of you. I thought which road would Lavelle and his ever so strange mother, if you don't mind me saying . . .

Lavelle   It's alright, she'll admit herself that she can be a little strange.

Jeremy   Which road would they have me travel? And I thought about my deceased parents and what road they would point to and I realised that I didn't want to travel down either of them. What's wrong with turning round and going right back? In that moment, that precise moment, I found what I'd been looking for my whole life. The strength to show the real me to the world. The strength to say no! You did that for me.

Lavelle   Did you bring me all the way down here to say this? Because trust me, I coulda left that five-eighty on my Oyster and you could have said it all on the phone.

Jeremy   Ahhhh, I'm feeling so ecstatically optimistic today. It's freedom. To think. Space, to think.

Lavelle   Maybe it wasn't so bad after all.

Jeremy   It's not the weed, fool. It's freedom. To think.

Lavelle *looks to* **Jeremy**.

Lavelle   My uncle used to say something like that when my mum cussed him about going foreign.

Jeremy *pulls an envelope out of his jacket pocket and hands it to* **Lavelle**.

Jeremy   I called you here for this . . . This is where your uncle is right now. Lawyers have seen him and the Foreign Office assure me that it is all under control and he will be back in London within a few days.

Lavelle   Yeah, really?

Jeremy   Not everything is done in the full glare of the public.

Lavelle *(reads)*   Oh wow. Oh, thank you, Jeremy. Thank you so much.

Jeremy   Thank Jennifer. She's the one that connected. I also bought a gift for you.

He pulls out of his bag a little wooden almost flute-like instrument.

Jeremy   You know what this is?

Lavelle   Ain't got the foggiest.

Jeremy   A replica of the Ishango bone. It's the first ever human chart of mathematical prime numbers! The earliest lunar calendar known to man kind. 6500 BC. They found it in Central Africa . . .

Lavelle   And you're giving that old ting to me – why?

Jeremy   Because it *time*, Lavelle. It's time to stop messing about. The old guard are dying and if we don't seize this moment, it will pass us by and we will die without anyone ever remembering that we were here. My mother's words to me . . . She was a bit weird too, actually! I also went to see your old head teacher this morning. Then I went to college round the corner from here and got these.

Lavelle   What are they?

Jeremy   Admission forms. Granted you're a bit late, but they can start you in January.

Lavelle   To do what?

Jeremy   A-levels of your choice and then on to a degree. I'm not messing about, Lavelle. The term that you've missed we can mug up together.

Lavelle (*gently*)   That stuff ain't doing nothing for me. I don't want to go to . . .

Jeremy   You have to! A mind like yours cannot be allowed to slip through the net. I told you once you were my gift – let me give you in return the courage to check back in.

He holds out the forms. After a good few beats **Lavelle** *takes them. But* **Jeremy** *doesn't let go.*

Lavelle   Out of respect for you I'm gonna take, um, out of your hands, but this isn't my road, J.

Jeremy   It's got to be, brother. It's the only road there is.

He lets go.

Lavelle   Like I said, out of respect.

Jeremy   This is the last of our official meetings, Lavelle, you know that, right?

Lavelle   Yep.

Jeremy   You wanna celebrate by coming out to eat with me and my girl?

Lavelle   Only if your chomping at KFC White City.

Jeremy   I can assure you we are not.

Lavelle   Then no, blud. You know I ain't gonna feel comfortable where you guys are gonna wanna go.

Jeremy   Alright, we go somewhere that you wanna go?

Lavelle   Na man, you roll wid your gal, yeah.

Jeremy   You gonna come see me again? I mean, you don't have to, there's no jailhouse hanging over your head. But I mean it when I say we can swot up together. Trust me, I ain't got anything better to do with my time bar sit back and listen to some old soul records.

Lavelle   I dunno. I got a feeling once my uncle's back he's gonna stick around for a bit so I might kinda hang with him.

Jeremy   OK.

Silence.

Lavelle   I'm gonna go now.

Jeremy   Yes, fine.

Lavelle   Thank you for my gift. My mum's gonna love it.

Jeremy   I thought she would.

Lavelle   Thank you, bruf.

Jeremy   My pleasure.

Lavelle *turns and walks away. He looks back once and then runs back towards* **Jeremy**.

Lavelle   Oh my days, I forgot I had a gift for you.

He pulls his hand out of his pocket and smacks **Jeremy** *full in the face.*

Lavelle (*laughing*)   Just had to get you back, bruf. We equal now, yeah?!

Jeremy (*laughs*)   You are so ghetto! . . . But yeah, now we equal.

Lavelle *walks off, smiling. After a few beats* **Susan** *appears.*

Susan   Did you give him the college papers?

Jeremy   Yep.

Susan   Is he?

Jeremy   All that's important is we planted the seed, right?

Susan   Maybe.

Jeremy   Wanna eat now? I'm starving.

Susan   Yeah, why not. My treat!

Jeremy   What you treating me for?

Susan   Cos I like you. Cos you my man now. Cos you jacked in the biggest job a black man's been offered. Cos you did the right thing but mostly cos you ain't got no job.

Jeremy   Oh yeah. There is that. But don't worry about me, I'm running for leader of the Labour Party tomorrow . . .

Susan   I like it – Jeremy Charles for Prime Minister.

Jeremy   Today London, tomorrow, the worlddddddddd!

They laugh as the lights come down. They stop before black out and snap back up.

You think I'm joking!

Lights.

Bola Agbaje

Detaining Justice

Bola Agbaje

Bola Agbaje was a member of the Young Writers' Programme
at the Royal Court Theatre and her first play, *Gone Too Far!*,
premiered there in February 2007. The production won a
2008 Olivier Award for Outstanding Achievement in an
Affiliate Theatre before transferring to the Royal Court
Theatre Downstairs in July 2007. Her other plays for theatre
include *Sorry Seems to be the Hardest Word* (Royal Court Tent at
Latitude, 2007), *Reap What You Sow* (Young Vic, 2007), *Rivers
Run Deep* (Hampstead Theatre, 2007), *Off the Endz* (Rough
Cuts, Royal Court, 2008), *Legend of Moremi* (Theatre Royal,
Stratford, 2008) and *Good Neighbours* (Talawa Unzipped at the
Young Vic, 2008). She is currently Pearson Playwright in
Residence for Paines Plough and is adapting *Gone Too Far!* into
a full-length screenplay for the UK Film Council and Poisson
Rouge Pictures.

Detaining Justice was first performed as part of the 'Not Black and White' season at the Tricycle Theatre, London, on 25 November 2009. The cast was as follows:

Mr Cole	Karl Collins
Chi Chi	Rebecca Scroggs
Grace	Sharon Duncan-Brewster
Justice	Aml Ameen
Abeni	Cecilia Noble
Pra	Kobna Holdbrook-Smith
Jovan *and* **Guard**	Rob Whitelock
Alfred	Jimmy Akingbola
Ben	Abhin Galeya
Guard *and* **Passer-by**	John Boyega

Director Indhu Rubasingham
Designer Rosa Maggiora
Lighting Designer James Farncombe
Sound Designer Tom Lishman
Costume Supervisor Sydney Florence
Production Manager Shaz McGee
Casting Suzanne Crowley and Gilly Poole

2009/10 new writing for new audiences supported by BLOOMBERG

Characters

Mr Cole, *lawyer, black male, thirty to forty. Well educated. English accent*

Chi Chi, *student, lawyer's assistant, black female, under twenty. English accent, speaks very fast*

Grace, *refugee, black female, twenty to thirty. Zimbabwean accent, quiet*

Justice, *asylum seeker, black male, twenty to thirty. Zimbabwean accent*

Abeni, *illegal immigrant, black female, thirty to forty. Nigerian accent, loud*

Pra, *illegal immigrant, black male, thirty to forty. Ghanaian accent*

Jovan, *immigrant cleaner, white male, thirty to forty*

Alfred, *Home Office case worker, black male, thirty to forty. English accent, arrogant, geeky, unattractive*

Ben, *Home Office enforcement officer, white male, twenty to thirty*

Guards 1 *and* **2**

Passer-by

Passengers 1 *and* **2**

Scene One

We are in a very small, cluttered office. It looks like a storage room, with boxes and rubbish littering the floor and desk. A small table is at the side with a kettle, tea and coffee. **Mr Cole**, *a black man in his thirties, is dressed in an expensive suit and looks very sharp. He is being shown round by* **Chi Chi**, *a young black lady in her early twenties. She gets out a box from the corner and begins to place old files in it.* **Chi Chi** *has a cockney accent and speaks really fast.* **Mr Cole** *stands and watches as she wanders around the room tidying up.*

Chi Chi   This over here is your desk. I know it a bit small, we can move some . . .

Mr Cole   It's quite alright.

Chi Chi   This is *not* one of my best inductions.

Mr Cole   It's fine.

Chi Chi   I actually thought it was a joke when they said you were coming here. When they asked me to prepare this room I thought I was being punked.

Mr Cole   Punked?

Chi Chi   Yeah, you know, ha ha, April Fools.

Mr Cole   Why is that?

Chi Chi   Because, you know, you are you! That guy that was in every newspaper in the country in January. The case is still fresh in everyone's mind. Even the other day we were all having a big row – well, not a row cos, you know, it wasn't your fault. Well, some people still think, erm . . . Did I say this here is your desk?

Mr Cole   Yes.

Chi Chi   Oh good . . . good!

Silence.

I wouldn't worry too much. You're in safe hands. I'm your biggest fan. And before you say it, I am not a stalker or nothing. I mean I don't know where you live . . . well, I know what area . . . but I've never been to your house.

Mr Cole (*replies cautiously*)   You know where I live?

Chi Chi   Yeah, it's on Google.

Mr Cole   Pardon?

Chi Chi   Every and anything you need to know about anyone that is anyone is on Google.

Mr Cole   My address?

Chi Chi   You mean to tell me you have never googled yourself?!

Mr Cole   No.

Chi Chi   There is about twenty pages just on you, not to talk about how many pages there is on the Johnson case. Hold on a minute. You do know how to use the internet, right?

Mr Cole   Course I do.

Chi Chi   You got me worried there, cos in this job the rules for immigration change every day. Internet is the only way for us to keep up.

Mr Cole   How do I get my details removed from the internet?

Chi Chi   You are so funny. Are you sure you know what the internet is?

Mr Cole   I'm not comfortable with my personal details being in the public realm.

Chi Chi *laughs.*

Mr Cole   I don't understand what's funny about that.

Chi Chi   You're not that famous, love, calm down. You're not gonna have paps queuing up outside your front door, and even so, if someone wanted to find you, the internet is not the only way to look. Once, right, my ex started seeing this really ugly girl and I wanted to know where she lived . . . not cos I was gonna do anything, I just wanted to know. So I called up the T-Mobile, pretended I was her, and before they got me confirming her address I got them to confirm it for me. Trust me, if you wanna find someone it's not hard. So about the Johnson case . . .

Mr Cole   Do you mind if we don't talk about it?

Chi Chi   Sorry, oh my gosh, sorry, I'm doing it again. I'm a bit too much. Everyone tell me that, my mum, my dad, my best mate Rach, cousins, aunts . . . It's just I am so nervous being here with you.

Mr Cole   It's fine . . .

Chi Chi   You are one of the best prosecuting lawyers in this country. *One of the best black lawyers* . . . and I can't believe you are here at the Immigration Advisory Centre. I'm really happy, *It's exciting!* We have always needed someone like you.

Mr Cole   Thank you!

Chi Chi   I do have one last question though.

Mr Cole   As long as it is not about the Johnson case.

Chi Chi   What made you wanna work here?

Mr Cole   I needed a change.

Chi Chi   You do know it's a step backwards?

Mr Cole   I wouldn't call it going backwards.

Chi Chi   You are *not* getting paid.

Mr Cole   Money is not always everything.

Chi Chi   I love it! Only someone with it will make a comment like that. If you got any spare I'm not too proud to beg, trust me.

She puts her hands out.

Mr Cole   You're not backward in coming forward, are you?

Chi Chi   Don't ask, you don't receive.

Mr Cole (*laughs*)   May I ask why you are here?

Chi Chi   I'm still studying and I need the experience.

Mr Cole   Do you enjoy your job?

Chi Chi   Sometimes.

Mr Cole   And the other times . . . ?

Chi Chi   If I am honest, it gets on my nerves. I mean, don't get me wrong, I like helping people. I love it. But I personally find that the cases we deal with are often beyond our control. But with you working with us now I'm guessing it's all gonna change.

Mr Cole   Hope so. I am impressed with the work that you do.

Chi Chi   Wow. Thank you.

She continues packing away the rubbish from the room.

Your induction will go a bit quicker if you join in.

She throws a black bag at him. **Mr Cole** *laughs.*

Chi Chi   A smile! So you are human.

Mr Cole *laughs again and begins to pick up litter from the floor.*

Mr Cole   Any chance of a cup of coffee while we work?

Chi Chi   Oh my gosh, I forgot.

She walks over to a desk with a kettle, tea, coffee, milk and sugar. She checks to see if there is water in the kettle and turns it on.

What would you like?

Mr Cole   Coffee, white with two sugar.

Chi Chi (*checks the containers*)   Yep, we got that.

She looks at **Mr Cole**. *He stares back.*

Silence.

Mr Cole   Oh, I need to . . . I thought that you . . .

He goes over to the table, picks up a mug and starts making his coffee.

Chi Chi   When I said this office is small, I meant to say it's a self-serving office. You make your own drinks, do your own photocopying, faxing, take your own calls, type your own letters, the post box is round the corner and –

Mr Cole   I get it.

Chi Chi   You want to go back to the Crown Court?

Mr Cole   Certainly not.

Chi Chi *goes over to a corner where a stack of files are lined up against the wall.*

Chi Chi   On that note, here is your first case.

Mr Cole*'s eyes lights up.*

Chi Chi   Kidding.

She picks up a small pile from the bunch.

Here.

Mr Cole (*takes the file and opens it*)   Mr Justice Ncube.

Chi Chi   He came to this country seeking asylum.

Mr Cole   What happened?

Chi Chi   He is being detained.

Mr Cole   What did he do?

Chi Chi   Enter the country illegally.

Scene Two

Across town, in a room at a detention centre. **Grace**, *a Zimbabwean refugee in her late twenties, is sitting on a chair, waiting impatiently. She goes over to the door and puts her ear to it, trying to listen for a sound. She gets nervous when she thinks she hears something, and runs back to her seat. She sits silently for a few moments and puts her head in her hands.*

The door opens. **Justice**, *her brother, who is in his mid-twenties, is standing there with a* **Guard***. He comes in. She stands up. He remains still. She remains still. The* **Guard** *exits and shuts the door.*

She runs to her brother. They both have Zimbabwean accents.

Justice   You look well.

Grace   Thank you.

Justice   How's everything?

Grace   I can't believe you are in here. I have been running around trying to find out what I need to do . . . I . . .

Justice   How is work?

Grace   Work? I can't think about that right now. I went to the Immigration Advisory Centre. They are going to deal with your case. They are waiting for a lawyer to start work and then –

Justice   How is your boyfriend?

Grace   What is your problem?

Justice   You are worrying for nothing. I will be fine.

Grace   I am going to go and see the lawyer tomorrow. I hope he will get you out.

Silence.

Your friends ask about you.

Justice   Tell them I miss them.

Grace   They are very lovely people.

Justice   Make sure you tell them I am doing well.

Grace   Pra keeps on inviting me to church.

Justice   Pastor Pra. He is alway recruiting.

Grace   I have not been to church in a very long time . . . not since Daddy's funer –

Justice   You should go.

Silence.

Grace   Are they feeding you?

Justice   These people can't cook.

Grace   Don't go making trouble, Justice.

Justice   I'm not. I have only told them, they should make me chef.

Grace   You can't cook.

Justice   I can cook better than you.

Grace   In your dreams.

Justice   When are you going to admit that I am the best in the family?

Grace   The day you find something to be better than me at. A monkey can boil rice.

Justice   At least I don't burn it.

Grace   *Once!*

Justice   Liar.

Grace   It only got burnt because I forgot about it.

Justice   Excuse!

Grace   I was cooking before you could walk.

Justice   So you say!

Grace   I have been preparing your meals since you was a baby.

Justice   And poisoning me in the process.

Grace   When have I poisoned you?

Justice   When I was ten – remember, as soon as I ate your stew I was throwing it all up. Dad have to rush me to the hospital.

Grace   Your memory is so short. Do you not remember before you ate the stew you were stuffing your face with chocolate and sweets?

Justice   Don't be mad, Grace.

Grace   I am not mad.

Justice   That is why your face is squashed like this. (*He demonstrates.*)

Grace   I just don't like it when you don't tell the story correctly.

Justice   It is not my fault God blessed me with the cooking skills. If you have a problem, take it up with Him.

Grace   Justice, you are a fool sometimes.

Justice   And you are a monkey.

Grace   Baboon.

Justice   Ape!

Grace   Me, an ape?!

Justice   Yes, look at your nose.

Grace   I have the perfect nose.

Justice   For an ape!

Grace   Why do you alway have to have the last word?

Justice   Why do you?

Grace   Because I am older.

Justice   But I am always right.

Grace   Do you think so?

Justice   I know!

Grace   What about the time we could not get the meat out of the freezer because it was stuck between all the ice. I told you we would need to switch it off and let the ice melt, but you decided to take a hammer to break the ice, and you broke the freezer.

They both start laughing.

Justice   Did I or did I not get the meat out?

Grace   As well as a beating from Daddy.

They laugh again.

Justice   He loved that freezer more than he loved us. Always wanted to be the first in town to have everything.

Grace   He just wanted to provide the best for his family. Things would be so different if our country was . . .

Justice   I know.

Grace   I miss him.

Justice   Me too.

Grace   Justice, I . . .

Justice   Don't. It will be –

Grace   *Don't say OK!* It is a mess. Zimbabwe fell apart around us and now you are locked up here like a caged animal . . .

Justice   Stop worrying.

Grace   How long are they going to keep you?

Justice   I don't know.

Grace   You should have waited. I would have applied for you to come here legally –

Justice   I will be out of here before you know it, and then we can have a cooking competition.

Grace *(begins to laugh)*   There is no competition.

Justice   It is the fear of losing to your junior brother that is making you talk like this.

Grace *gives her brother a kiss on the cheek.*

Grace   This is what I love about you, Justice.

Justice   What?

Grace   You don't give in till you win.

Justice   Life is too short, my sister.

They hug each other tightly.

Scene Three

The next day.

We are in the station cleaners' lunch room. **Pra** *is sitting in a corner. He is trying to write a letter but is finding it difficult to start.* **Abeni** *enters. She puts down her bag, takes out a takeaway container and heads for the sink. The sink is full of dishes. She looks around for a clean plate but does not find one. She takes off her jewellery and begins to wash the plates in the sink.*

Abeni   Look at this place.

Pra   Is that how you say hello?

Abeni   Every day when I want to eat I have to tidy up after you animals.

Pra   Who are you calling an animal? Is it my rubbish?

Jovan *enters the room, extremely angry and upset.*

Jovan   I hate this country.

Pra   Hello to you too.

Jovan   Why does everything have to be so hard?

Abeni   What happened?

Jovan   What do I tell my family?

Pra   Answer de woman, what happened?

Jovan   He has done it again.

Abeni   Who?

Jovan   The man who owns the papers I am using.

Pra   You can't say I didn't warn you.

Jovan   Thank you very much!

Pra   I told you it was not a good idea.

Abeni   How can you tell someone what he did is not a good idea, when you was not there the day he choose to do it?

Pra   Who is talking to you, foolish woman?

Abeni   Abi, you own my mouth?

Jovan   People, what am I going to do?

Pra   Jovan, there is nothing you can do.

Jovan   The man has my money.

Abeni   Can't you speak to his wife?

Pra   Of course, his wife will tell him to give Jovan back his money. It is not like she would not benefit from it. You are sooo wise, Abeni. Are you related to Einstein?

Jovan   What?

Pra   Don't listen to her. What is his wife going to do?

Abeni   Do you have a better idea?

Pra   Yes. (*To* **Jovan**.) You have to find someone else's papers to use.

Abeni   Stupid idea.

Pra   Better than your own. This is not the first time this man has done this to you. Last month he didn't give you your money because he said he didn't receive it, although you showed him your payslip. This month what is his excuse?

Jovan   The bank took it because he went over his overdraft.

Abeni   Ahhh.

She shakes her head, disappointed.

Pra   When you told me he said he would do it for free,
I knew it was a lie. No clone will ever let someone use their
name, their details, for free. He knew he was going to benefit
from this right from day one. You are giving your money
away.

Jovan   Maybe I should go to the police.

Pra *and* **Abeni**   AHHH!

Pra   Are you mad?

Abeni   Have you lost your mind?

Pra   Police!

Abeni   Have you bumped your head?

Pra   Abeni, speak to him-o.

Abeni   Pra, tell him.

Pra   He wants to go to the police.

Abeni   Please God put some sense into him.

Pra   Come, let us pray.

He tries to hold **Jovan**'*s hand.* **Jovan** *pushes him away.*

Jovan   I am not in the mood.

Abeni   Before they go looking for him they will arrest you.
You are not meant to be in this country.

Pra *and* **Abeni**   Have you forgotten?

Pra   Police is the last people you need to see.

Jovan   He has my money. I can't eat, I can't pay my rent.
I can't send money home. What am I going to do?

After **Abeni** *finishes with the dishes, she gets out a cloth and begins to
wipe down the tables, placing the litter that has been left around the room
in the bin.*

Pra   I have a friend.

Abeni   You always have a friend.

Pra   Woman, I am only going to tell you this once.

Abeni   Tell me what?

Pra   Shut up your mouth.

Abeni   Do you own me? As I have told you many a times, outside church you are no longer the pastor. You are just Pra.

Pra   You have no respect.

Jovan   People, I need help!

Pra   Don't mind her, I was saying I have a friend who can sort this out. I can get you your own papers.

Abeni   If that is the case, how come you don't have your own papers?

Pra   Shut up!

Abeni   You say that to me again and I will slap that dirty mouth of yours.

Pra   You want to fight me?

Abeni   I will not fight you, I will beat you.

Pra   Beat me then, and see if God don't strike you.

Abeni   He will strike you first. Jovan, listen, all you can do, my brother, is try and reason with this guy. It is not like you can come to work tomorrow with a new name, new passport. You are stuck with de man's details. Maybe you should ask him if he can open a new bank account and he can give you the card and PIN and . . .

Pra   Sometimes you are stupider than stupid.

Abeni   And you are smart?

Pra   Why would he do that?

Abeni   How long have you been in this country?

Pra   Longer than you!

Abeni   And you still don't know nothing. (*To* **Jovan**.)
Anything is worth a try. Just tell him you are willing to pay
him a fee. He can even set up a standing order so he can have
the money the day you get paid. You are at his mercy, you
have to play by his rules.

Pra   Nonsense! My friend can –

Jovan   She is right. I am stuck with this man. I am stuck
with the name Jovan.

He puts his head on the table.

Abeni *goes over to her bag. She takes out ten pounds and hands it to
him.* **Jovan** *does not take it. She offers it again.*

Jovan   I will pay you back.

Abeni   Don't worry. God always provides.

Pra   First sensible thing to come out of your mouth.

Jovan   What are you writing?

Pra   A character reference for Justice.

Abeni   Why are you writing it?

Pra   It will help support his case.

Abeni   They are not going to take it seriously from you.

Pra   And why not?

Abeni   They do not see you as a citizen.

Pra   I am a pastor. A man of honour.

Abeni   Illegal honour.

Pra   Who asked you?

Jovan   I don't like this place.

Abeni   Just remember why you are here.

Pra   Keep counting your blessings.

Abeni   You could be locked in a detention centre, like
Justice.

Jovan   Why is it such a crime to want a better life?

Abeni   Because you want it in this country.

Jovan   British people are selfish.

Abeni   It is not the people, it is the government. If that stupid man Tony Blair –

Pra   – Gordon Brown.

Abeni   They are all the same. They think they know what this country needs. But what they don't know is that they need us.

She finishes tidying up. She washes her hands and takes her takeaway container over to the microwave. She places her food in the microwave.

Pra   Why are you shouting?

Abeni   Who are you talking to?

Pra   You are getting on my nerves, giving me head pains.

Abeni   Close your ears. I was talking to Jovan.

Pra   Jovan has enough on his plate. He does not need to hear the nonsense you say day in day out right now.

Abeni   If Jovan does not want to listen, he has a mouth to say so.

She looks at **Jovan***.*

Abeni   Do you want me to be quiet?

Jovan *does not respond.*

Abeni   Eh-eh. I will not talk to any of you two.

Jovan   Don't be like that, Abeni, I just have . . .

The food is ready. **Abeni** *takes it out of the microwave, goes to a seat at a table and begins to eat.*

Pra   Leave her. She needs to be quiet. Let her concentrate on eating her smelly food in the corner.

Abeni   You are mad.

Pra   I have warned you before to stop bringing in that dish. That is not jollof rice.

Abeni   And how would you know? This is a traditional Nigerian dish.

Pra   It is Ghanaian!

Abeni   De devil has possessed you. Your people came to my country to learn this dish because all your other food is rubbish.

Pra   It's a lie!

Abeni   You are foolish. I have seen the way your women cook this . . . basmati rice is not for jollof. Stupid man!

Pra   Stop talking to me.

He puts his hands to his ears.

Abeni   Aaaaa! Listen, I am not your mate.

Pra   LEAVE ME ALONE!

Jovan   Why does it always turn into argument with you two?

Abeni   He has no respect!

Pra   I respect human being.

Jovan   Tomorrow at church you two will be best of friends.

Scene Four

Two weeks later. **Mr Cole** *is settled in the office. He is now dressed casually. The files on the floor have been cleared. He is typing on the computer.* **Chi Chi** *is at a small fax machine. She dials a number and places a piece of paper in the machine. The fax is sent.*

Chi Chi   It seems to be working OK.

Mr Cole   What can I say? You have magical fingers.

Chi Chi   Do I now?

She crosses her arms and looks at **Mr Cole**. *He senses her gaze and looks up from his desk.*

Mr Cole   What?

He smiles.

Chi Chi   I am not a PA.

Mr Cole   Whoever said you were? Can you make me a cuppa?

Chi Chi's *mouth drops.*

Mr Cole   Calm down. It's a joke. I'm kidding.

He gets up, goes over to the desk with the kettle and switches it on.

Would you like one?

Chi Chi   No.

Mr Cole *laughs.*

Chi Chi   It's not funny. I am not your PA.

Mr Cole   I know.

Chi Chi   I hope you do, cos if the printer is out of ink or the paper is jammed or the computer freezes or the electricity goes out or the door is stuck or the phone does not dial out, Chi Chi is not a mechanic.

Mr Cole (*laughs*)   Mechanic? Don't you mean technician?

Chi Chi   Same difference.

Mr Cole   It's not.

Chi Chi   I don't care. We are not at the Old Bailey.

Mr Cole   Give me a break, I am trying here.

Chi Chi   You need to try a bit harder.

Mr Cole   I'm sorry, you are right.

Chi Chi   Apology accepted. How is the Justice Ncube case going? His sister has been coming in and out of this place like it is her second home.

Mr Cole   I know, I met her the other day. I've booked an appointment to –

Chi Chi   When?

Mr Cole   The 27th.

Chi Chi   The 27th? That's too far away. You need to change it to this week.

She goes over to her desk. There is a box on the floor filled with papers. She begins to file the papers in a nearby cabinet.

Mr Cole   It was the earliest date they had.

Chi Chi   That's what they like to say, but you have to tell them it an emergency.

Mr Cole   Will do.

Chi Chi   Pick up the phone and call them now.

Mr Cole   I will call them later.

Chi Chi   You don't want him to get lost in the system, cos that happens all the time, you know.

Mr Cole   I understand. But I'm dealing with the prick of the century at the Home Office.

He finishes making his coffee and heads over to his desk.

Chi Chi   Who?

Mr Cole   Alfred Thomas.

Chi Chi   Alfred? Then you definitely need to get a move on. He going to –

Mr Cole   I am putting a request in for a PA.

Chi Chi   In your dreams, love. I can support you as much as I can. But you have a lot of work to do. Our clients are fighting to stay and their lives are in your hands.

Mr Cole   I can handle it.

Chi Chi   I'm not saying you can't handle it. I'm just saying you got to be fast, quick off the mark. Like calling back now to get a better appointment date and then calling Alfred to make sure he has all the relevant paperwork. The Home Office has a habit of losing documents.

Mr Cole *rolls his eyes and goes over to the phone. He picks up a card and dials the number.*

Mr Cole   Engaged!

Chi Chi   Keep trying! I know I'm going on at you, but this is what we have to do to get results. If it was really up to me, the one advice I want to give our clients is to stop fighting and go back to their homes. This country is not that great. The roads aren't paved with gold, it's concrete, tarmac and potholes.

Mr Cole *keeps redialling the number. He gets no answer and puts the phone down.*

Mr Cole   What you and I class as riches is not what many of them are searching for.

Chi Chi   But they all come here looking for a better life, don't they?

Mr Cole   Indeed!

Chi Chi   So there you go.

Mr Cole   Be that as it may, it is not always for material gains. What is your life aim?

Chi Chi   To be an excellent lawyer.

Mr Cole *continues dialling, but the number is still engaged.*

Mr Cole   What if the government puts restrictions on you fulfilling your full potential and –

Chi Chi   They do.

Mr Cole   By what means?

Chi Chi   Student loans!

Mr Cole   Point taken. Nonetheless if you wanted to go to university, by taking up the student loan, you could. You have many options. Can you imagine if you lost that freedom, that choice?

Chi Chi *shakes her head.*

Mr Cole   In some countries there is no such thing as freedom. Some people flee from terrible situations . . . persecutions . . .

He goes over to the photocopying machine and begins to take copies from a law book.

Chi Chi   But that's the thing, they come to be persecuted here! I'm not disputing that some people have it hard. I'm just saying the weather alone here makes me depressed to the point where all I wanna do is stay in bed and bawl my eyes out. It is *unpredictable*! The constant sunshine in Africa should make them want to stay there. The sun makes me happy. Imagine waking up every day with the sun beating down on your face . . .

Mr Cole   Earth to Chi Chi, are you in there? Not all immigrants are from Africa, and –

Chi Chi   I know, I know. It sound like I am talking crazy, but I don't know of *any* asylum seekers or immigrant who feels they can call this place their home.

Mr Cole   That can't be true.

Chi Chi *goes back to the fax machine and picks up a file she left on the side. She hands it to* **Mr Cole**.

Chi Chi   It's true. Here, look at the review I did today. That guy there, Frank, could not wait to get his stay. He was so desperate for it. Once he was told that he was going to get it he was so excited. He offered to take the whole office out for lunch. He thought that he was going to start a brand new life. You could not rub the smile off his face. But today when he came down he was miserable, sad and lonely. I didn't even recognise him at first, he had lost so much weight. He was begging to go back home. He hadn't found a job and he got beaten up two week ago just for a laugh cos of his accent. He couldn't stop crying.

Mr Cole   It takes a while for people to adapt.

Chi Chi   *But it's not about adapting!* It's about acceptance and as much as this country goes on that they are accepting and how welcoming it is . . . it is not. If you ask me, the dodgy politicians chat absolute bollocks about Britishness and multi-whatever-you-want-to-call-it. It really gets to me sometimes. People here have this hatred towards asylum seekers, immigrants, and for what? Honestly, I'm telling them to go home to their countries cos I care. This country is bloody racist!

Mr Cole *finishes with the photocopying machine and heads back to his desk.*

Mr Cole   What I have learnt from it is to rise above it.

Chi Chi   Easier said than done, I mean, just last week I was driving, right, and I was trying to park –

Mr Cole   Women drivers . . .

He picks up the phone to try the detention centre again.

Chi Chi   Oi, you. I can drive . . . Anyways, I didn't see this car, it came from nowhere, and the stupid driver instead of waiting, he beeps his horns. Beeps his horn, you know. All I said to him was, 'Can you be patient, please?' and the next thing I know he winds down the window and shouts, 'Get out the way, you stupid black cow.' I mean, why couldn't I just be a cow? Why do I have to be a black cow? I could have been a yellow cow, a blue cow, a green cow, but nooo, he wants to call me a black cow. I swear cows are even black and white, not just one colour.

Mr Cole   Presumably you responded.

Chi Chi   I told him, shut your mouth, you stupid white cunt.

Mr Cole   Chi Chi!

Chi Chi   Yeah, trust me. He is not gonna call me a black cow and get away with it. I will give as good as I get cos I know I have every right to be here. This place just gets me angry.

Mr Cole   Anger is good. It makes you fight for something.

Chi Chi   No, it just makes my forehead wrinkle. I bet when I'm older I'm going to have to have Botox and bloody plastic surgery to get rid of these lines. I would love to start a campaign, you know – stay away from England. Grass is not greener.

Mr Cole   The reality is, the majority of the time this country is better than the one they are fleeing from.

Chi Chi   No.

Mr Cole   Come on.

Chi Chi (*reluctantly gives in*)   OK. Maybe I just hate the rules then. My mum was telling me, right, did you know there was a time that Britain went out and colo – What's that word again.

Mr Cole   Colonised?

Chi Chi   Yeah, colonised counties, you know, went about the world and took over. The great British Empire, you know . . . who the hell do they think they are? They made it OK for all their people to go round the world and set up home, and even if the frigging people who were there first disagreed it didn't matter! They fought them to take over and now when people want to come here they create barriers and rules to stop people from doing the same. But that don't stop them importing our food and selling it in supermarkets. Imagine if all foreign countries said that they were not going to sell any vegetables and fruits, how will this country survive? Most of their food is from foreign export, mate. Don't you believe that people should be allowed to do what they want? The world doesn't belong to any one person or any one race.

Mr Cole   I agree with you. Everyone should have the right to freedom of movement, and to an extent people do. We are all free to move about within our country's borders.

Chi Chi If I wanted to go to Alaska, I shouldn't have to ask anyone.

Mr Cole Thought you liked the sunshine.

Chi Chi I'm just saying.

Mr Cole I wish life was that simple, my dear.

Chi Chi It should be. If I wanted to go to the moon, I should be able to get in my spaceship and blast off into the distance without having anyone's permission. What happened to being free?

Mr Cole Democracy says we are free but in reality it is far from the case. Free world is an unrealistic fantasy.

Chi Chi I'm definitely free.

Mr Cole You park that precious car of yours on a double yellow line and see how fast you will get a ticket, clamped or, worst, get towed. Then tell me what happens when you refuse to pay the fines or pick up your car from the pound.

Chi Chi OK, you got a point there!

Mr Cole How can we be free if there are laws imposed on us? Even the term 'freedom of speech' is not really free. There are restrictions on the things we can and can't say.

Chi Chi Not me, mate. I will say what I want when I want. Ain't no one the boss of me apart from me!

Mr Cole I really love your innocence. A word to the wise though, since the Universal Declaration of Human Rights even the ideology of a free nation state has been one that cannot be obtained.

Chi Chi Erm, English, Mr Cole.

Mr Cole I am speaking English.

Chi Chi Not my English. What are you on about?

Mr Cole Article 5 of the Universal Declaration of Human Rights is: no one shall be subjected to torture or to cruel, inhuman or degrading treatment or punishment. Right?

Chi Chi   I don't know. I've never read it.

Mr Cole   So you take my word for it?

Chi Chi   I'm gonna have to, ain't I?

Mr Cole   How many countries do you know that stick to this article?

Chi Chi   You want me to count?

Mr Cole   No. I am asking do you know of any country in this world that treats all its people fairly – and when I mean fairly, I mean equally.

Chi Chi   I don't know, you're confusing me.

Mr Cole   What I'm trying to say to you is there is no such thing as a free person. Freedom is measured differently from country to country, and this country is comparatively better. This is the reason people want to come here.

Chi Chi   Fine, you may be right. But I'm still starting my campaign.

Mr Cole   Go ahead. Despite the fact that you dislike the British Empire for colonising many nations, it can be argued that if the British still stayed in many of these poor counties then they wouldn't be as bad as they are today. Don't you at least agree that white people are more superior, more intelligent? They get things done. Keep the world moving.

Chi Chi   What?

Mr Cole   WWF . . .

Chi Chi   What is that?

Mr Cole   White Way Forward. Brings about development.

Chi Chi   Pardon me?

Mr Cole   As much as we dislike laws and rules they bring stability. You have to give credit to Western society, to the white man, for the rule of law.

At this point **Chi Chi** *stops what she is doing completely and jumps out of her seat.* **Mr Cole** *laughs.*

Chi Chi   NO WAY! THAT'S A LIE! In Africa we had laws!

Mr Cole   Yo, Black Panther! Calm down . . . when Chi Chi gets going she doesn't stop, does she?

Chi Chi (*laughs*)   Yeah, that right. White Way Forward? Bull! Africa was not a lawless nation. We had traditional laws.

Mr Cole   Which at times went against people's human rights.

Chi Chi   Mr Cole, you are starting to get on my nerves now. What is your issue with Africa? Africa was a beautiful nation before the invader went there to mess it up. But they do not want you to know all what I am telling you, trust me. The truth will –

Mr Cole   It doesn't always set you free.

Chi Chi   Like hell is does.

Mr Cole *is silent. He zones out for a while. Then:*

Mr Cole   Knowing the truth can tear you apart. It can ruin lives.

Chi Chi   What?

Mr Cole (*realising he had gone off on one*)   Nothing – forget it.

Chi Chi   You can't just say something like that and leave it.

Mr Cole   I said forget it. I need to get back to work, and so do you.

Chi Chi   You are weird sometimes, you know that? How does your wife put up with you? You suffer more mood swings than a woman on her reds.

She picks up her file and goes towards the door. **Mr Cole**'s *phone rings. He looks at it, it keeps ringing.* **Chi Chi** *stops and turns round.*

Chi Chi   Are you waiting for me to answer it?

Mr Cole *sighs and picks it up. He tries to talk in a whisper.*

Mr Cole   Yes . . . I am at work . . . I can't talk now . . .
I don't want to talk now . . . Can you not fucking hear me,
Diane? I said I do not want to talk now. When I wanted to
talk did you want to listen? . . . I will call you after five!

He slams the phone down.

Chi Chi   Hope that's not a client.

She begins to laugh.

Mr Cole   Sometimes you need to know when to put a cork
in it!

Chi Chi   Well, excuse me for breathing. Instead of switching
on me you should be trying to redial the detention centre so
you can go and see your client and chase up Alfred from the
Home Office.

She storms out. **Mr Cole** *gets up to go after* **Chi Chi** *but decides
otherwise. He takes out some antidepressants from his drawer and
swallows four pills. He goes over to the beverage table and starts to
prepare a coffee.*

Scene Five

The same day, in the Home Office. **Alfred**, *an immigration caseworker
in his mid-thirties, is at his desk going through some paperwork, while his
friend* **Ben**, *an enforcement officer, is telling him a story.*

Ben   Brother, let me tell you, that girl's badonkadonk was
just fantastic! Umm!

Alfred   You and a woman's bottom.

Ben   It was a feast. I enjoyed myself.

Alfred   If you put as much effort and energy that you put
into a woman's bottom into your work . . . you would get
some done!

Ben   Jealousy is a deadly sin. You get me?

Alfred   You get *me*?

Ben   My next-door neighbour say it at the time. Get me.

Alfred   He is child.

Ben   He is twenty-one and he send the buff girls my way. Get me?!

Ben *goes to give* **Alfred** *a high-five, and leaves him hanging.* **Alfred** *shakes his head.*

Alfred   Why do you have a wife if you love playing the field?

Ben   A man was never built for one woman. Monogamy is an English invention.

Alfred   Does your wife know your opinion on monogamy?

Ben   My wife has no say in what I think, seeing as I have no say in what she can think. We have an understanding she can do what she wants as long as she does not complain when I do my own thing. She is always quick to tell me I cannot think for her, cannot speak for her – it work both ways. Women of today always want to talk about –

Ben *and* **Alfred**   – independence!

They both laugh. A fax comes through on the machine. **Alfred** *goes to pick it up. He looks at it and rolls his eyes, places it on top of his pile.*

Ben   I am hungry. Can we go get some lunch, please? I am feeling some curry goat and rice.

Alfred   I got to get working on this case. I hate these bloody lawyers who want to throw their weight around. Who does this Cole guy think he is?!

Ben   What did he do?

Alfred   He wants me to call him about this stupid case. He can wait. I will call him when I am good and ready. I'm sick of this job.

Ben It's not that bad.

Alfred Says the enforcement officer.

Ben Enforcement is not as glamorous as you think.

Alfred It's better than this. I'm fed up of people wanting to drag out cases.

Ben Chill, bredwin!

Alfred That is not cool!

Ben What! Your people did not make up the word 'bredwin'. You heard of Shakespeare?

Alfred You heard of 'I don't care'?

Ben Come, we go.

Alfred I'm busy!

Ben You need a holiday.

Alfred Holiday is the last thing on my mind. I need to get this case out of the way. I'm making sure this guy goes back to his country.

Ben What did he do to you?

Alfred What do they always lie about?

Ben I don't know, most people I meet are genuine.

Alfred *shakes his head and gives* **Ben** *a dirty look.*

Alfred We will not even discuss the fact that it is *actually* your job to spot things like this.

Ben Like what?

Alfred He came through the borders with a fake passport.

Ben Oi, some of those copies are great replicas. I'm even thinking of setting up my own passport-cloning business. Do you know how much money is in that?

Alfred You should watch what you say – people round here don't take things like that as a joke.

Ben   Who's joking?

He takes **Justice**'s *passport and picks up a stamp from the table.* **Alfred** *snatches the stamp out of his hand.*

Alfred   What you doing?

Ben   Sorting out this case.

Alfred   This guy is not staying in this country. I am sending him back to where he belongs.

Ben   Why?

Alfred   It took him six months to come to our office to seek asylum.

Ben   Have you given him a chance to explain?

Alfred   I know all their tricks. He probably tried to get himself a job and found it difficult with no documents and thought the easiest thing would be to claim asylum. Well, not on my watch. He cannot prove his claim, and now that his case has been rejected he wants to give me trouble.

Ben   His country did go through a tough time.

Alfred   Trust me, I've seen this before. It's the oldest trick in the book.

Ben   Cut him a break.

Alfred   'Cut him a break'! You bump your head. If I took information like this as the gospel, I would be granting *every* asylum seeker leave to enter. You know it as well as I do, it is not that simple.

Ben   Better you than me.

The phone rings. **Alfred** *looks at the caller display. He walks away.* **Ben** *goes to pick it up and* **Alfred** *stops him.*

Alfred   What are you doing?

Ben   It's ringing!

Alfred   Ignore it.

Ben   Why?

Alfred   It's that lawyer at the IAC, the one I was just talking about.

Ben   How do you know that?

Alfred   I know that number – they bombard me with calls at least ten times a day. I only just got his fax. He needs to understand he can't just click his fingers and expect me to jump.

Ben   You take your job too seriously.

Alfred   *You* don't take it seriously enough. Watch when your daughter grows up and she need to look for a job. She is not going to stand a chance because all these damn immigrants would have come here and taken over. If it was up to you, these bloody lawyers and left-wing do-gooders, I bet you'd grant every asylum seeker not just leave to enter but free medical care and housing. Then when your daughter has no job, no house and has to queue for ten hours in the hospital you will only have yourself to blame with your soft approach and equal rights bullshit.

Ben   I don't have to worry about that. My daughter is getting sent back to India. Education system is better there. You are taking your frustration out on one guy. You have a lot of paperwork here. Just give him what he wants.

Alfred   It's not enough. He can't come here with his good looks and charm and think he gonna win me over. He have to demonstrate how he has been directly affected.

Ben   He's a member of the MDC.

Alfred   So?

Ben   He's written here, he is an active member.

Alfred   So what? I could be an active member of the BNP.

Ben   They would never accept you.

Alfred   What I am trying to say is, if I was a member of the BNP and I wanted to seek –

Ben   Why you using the BNP?

Alfred   It's an example.

Ben   But I don't get it.

Alfred   Shut up and I shall explain.

Ben   Use another example.

Alfred   I am using this one!

Ben   You are black. I could never believe you would be a member.

Alfred   The point is not about being a member.

Ben   What is the point?

Alfred   LET ME FINISH!

Ben   Do you honestly have a point?

Alfred   OK, fine! *If* a member of the BNP came and said that he needed asylum –

Ben   – *in England!*

Alfred   Hypothetically speaking.

Ben   They would never need to seek asylum.

Alfred   *That is not the point.*

Ben   A minute ago you said being a *member* wasn't the point.

Alfred   *It is not.*

Ben   How can seeking asylum not be the point too?

Alfred   What?

Ben   What is the point of this conversation?

Alfred   An asylum seeker has to provide a lot of evidence to back up their claim.

Ben   But you cannot even give an example of what evidence you are looking for.

Alfred   *I can!*

Ben   You were talking about the BNP.

Alfred   As an example!

Ben   A really rubbish one.

Alfred   I can't be bothered any more.

Ben   Are you sulking?

Alfred   You didn't let me speak.

Ben   Go on.

Alfred   Forget it!

Ben   Big baby.

Alfred   *You keep interrupting!*

Ben   I am trying to make sense of why you are using that example.

Alfred   Because it is just that. *An example.*

Ben   I'm not comfortable with it. You are black, you should find it even more uncomfortable than me. Use another one.

Alfred   I forgot what I was trying to say now.

Ben   I asked you why this guy . . . what's his name?

Alfred   Justice Ncube.

Ben   Justice? With a name like that you can't –

Alfred   It's all part of his act! I bet you someone back in his country advised him to change his name to that. Probably figured he will get more sympathy. Not with me.

Ben   I am hungry.

Alfred   Go get something to eat, because you are getting on my nerves.

Ben   I was waiting for you.

Alfred   Wait in silence!

Ben   Finish your story.

Alfred   I DON'T WANT TO.

Ben   I really would like to know where you are going with this.

Alfred   Did you not go through any training? In order to seek asylum a person has to show that they were being persecuted in their country and that they went to seek some help. But the ruling party – i.e. the government or the police – did nothing to protect them because a, they were a member themselves, or b, they support what they did and the only option was to seek asylum in another country.

Ben   This guy has here he was attacked – tortured to be precise. Look at the picture –

He hands **Alfred** *a picture of* **Justice**.

Ben   – because of the party he supported.

Alfred   I am not objecting or disputing that he was attacked but he has yet to prove that his only option was to flee the country. He was living in an area where his party was a minority. What stopped him from going to another part of the country where his party was the majority?

Ben   He may not have been able to get out of the area.

Alfred   He got far enough, he came to this country.

Ben   The police and the government at the time he fled were the opposing side.

Alfred   But not any more. They had an election a couple of months ago. His party is now in power.

Ben   Doesn't mean the country has changed.

Alfred   The bottom line still remains, he need to find a way to corroborate that leaving the country was his only option . . . and with all the evidence he's got here it is not enough. Only a few are affected but everyone wants to use political asylum as an excuse. Not going to wash with me!

Ben   Man, you are harsh.

Alfred   It's not my rules.

Ben   You take your job too seriously.

Alfred   I said before I wouldn't have to if you did yours.

Ben *picks up a copy of the case file and picks up a picture of* **Grace**.

Ben   Damn! Is this his wife?

Alfred (*snatches the picture*)   No, this is his sister.

Ben   She is *fiiinnne*!

Alfred   Give it back.

Ben   I'd love to meet her, sweeter the berry . . .

Alfred   Hands off, mate.

Ben   What do you mean, hands off . . . ?

He begins to howl like a wolf.

Alfred   Quiet, man.

Ben   You cannot hold a wild animal down. My gosh. Is she in this country? You cannot send her back.

Alfred   Her claim was accepted.

Ben   How does that work out?

Alfred   She was able to prove her case.

Ben   I am sure she did.

Alfred   Don't look at me like that. I didn't work on her case.

Ben   Bet you wish you did. She is *hot*. Do you have her number?

He picks up the rest of the file to search for it.

Alfred   Give it back!

Ben   Why are you trying to stop nature in its track?

Alfred   Stop nature in it tracks?

Ben   It is obvious she was destined to meet me.

Alfred   I recall when you met your current wife, you said she was destined to meet you.

He snatches the picture. The phone rings again. **Alfred** *looks at the caller display and ignores it.*

Scene Six

The stage has transformed into a church. **Pastor Pra**, *Ghanian with an African accent, enters onstage dressed in a 'kenke'. The* **Congregation** *follows closely behind, including* **Abeni**, *dressed in traditional African attire,* **Jovan** *in a suit and* **Grace** *in casual dress.* **Jovan** *and* **Abeni** *are enjoying the service and look comfortable and in their element, dancing along to the music.* **Grace** *looks out of place and a little lost.*

Pra   Oh Lord, once again we come into your presence, into your home, because we know you are going to bless us. So we lift our hands and we give you glory. Come on, people, let us praise the Lord.

The **Congregation** *gets up, cheers and begins to sing around the stage.*

Congregation
  We lift our hands in the sanctuary,
  We lift our hands to give you the glory,
  We lift our hands to give you the praise,
  And we will praise you for the rest of our days, yes!
  We will praise you for the rest of our days!

  We clap our hands in the sanctuary,
  We clap our hands to give you the glory,
  We clap our hands to give you the praise,
  And we will praise you for the rest of our days. Yes!
  We will praise you for the rest of our days!

  Jesus! We give you the praise!
  Emmanuel, we lift up your name!
  Heavenly father! Coming Messiah!
  And we will praise you for the rest of our days! Yes!
  We will praise you for the rest of our days! Yes!

The song ends. The **Congregation** *claps and they begin to take their seats.* **Abeni** *shouts at the top of her lungs.*

Abeni   We will praise you God. We will lift up your name!

Congregation   Hallelujah!

They all take their seat while **Pastor Pra** *remains standing.*

Pra   That is right, my people, we will praise the Lord for the rest of our days. CAN I GET AN AMEN!

Congregation   AMEN!

Grace *remains silent.*

Pra   I do not think the Lord can hear you. I SAID, CAN I GET AN AMEN!

Congregation   AMEN!

Pra   Grace, you are very quiet. Can I get an amen?

Grace   Amen.

Pra   *Yes. Yes.* We have to give thanks and praise at every opportunity. Beginning today and running through the month of December we are going to discover what it means to have faith for everyday living. I want to try to help you to discover what faith is, and how it can help you in your struggle to be everything that you can be in Christ.

Abeni *jumps out of her seat.*

Abeni   PRAISE THE LORD!

Pra   Hallelujah. Today, we simply want to get a grasp on what faith is. I am going to share a story with you.

A tourist came too close to the edge of the Grand Canyon, lost his footing and plunged over the side, clawing and scratching to save himself. After he went out of sight and just before he fell into space, he stumbled upon a scrubby bush which he desperately grabbed with both hands. Filled with terror, he called out towards heaven: 'Is there anyone up there?'

A calm, powerful voice came out of the sky: 'Yes, there is.'

The tourist pleaded: 'Can you help me? Can you help me?'

The calm voice replied: 'Yes, I probably can. What is your problem?'

'I fell over the cliff and I am dangling in space holding to a bush that is about to break. Please help me.'

The voice from above said: 'I'll try. Do you believe?'

'Yes, yes, I believe.'

Congregation *claps.*

Pra   'Do you have faith?'

'Yes, yes. I have strong faith.'

Congregation *claps again.*

Abeni   Have faith-o.

Pause.

Pra   The calm voice said: 'Well, in that case, simply let loose of the bush and everything will turn out fine.'

There was a tense pause, then the tourist yelled: 'Is there anyone else up there?'

Congregation *laughs, except* **Grace**.

Pra   You find it funny, my people, but it not a joking matter. It's one thing to talk about faith – it's quite another to act on faith.

Jovan *jumps out of his seat.*

Jovan   THAT IS RIGHT, PASTOR!

Abeni   You speak the truth-o!

Pra   Can I get an amen!

Congregation   AMEN!

Abeni (*to* **Grace**)   Come on, join in, my sister.

Grace   It's just –

Pra   Now turn to your neighbour and tell them, 'I have faith.'

They all turn to each other. **Grace** *is the only one who remains not convinced.*

Congregation   I have faith.

Abeni (*to* **Grace**)   Have faith-o.

Pra   We need God to hear us. I said, turn to your neighbour and tell them – I HAVE FAITH!

Congregation   I HAVE FAITH!

Pra *begins to sing. The* **Congregation** *gets up and begins to sing and dance along. Clapping their hands.*

Pra
    We are saying thank you, Jesus.

Congregation
    Thank you, my Lord.

Pra
    We are saying thank you, Jesus.

Congregation
    Thank you, my Lord.

They continue to sing the song.

Pra   I got a feeling that everything is going to be alright.

He goes up to **Grace** *and gives her a hug. She does not return it.*

Pra   The divine word has told me everything is going to be alright.

Abeni   Amen!

Jovan   Amen!

He gives **Abeni** *a hug.* **Pastor Pra** *walks around the* **Congregation** *hugging people.*

Pra Don't look at me, look beyond me for help. Whatever you want, God has said it is yours to receive.

Abeni *and* **Jovan** *scream out.*

Abeni   I RECEIVE IT!

Jovan   I RECEIVE IT TOO!

Pra *points the mike to* **Grace**.

Pra   Do you receive it?

He looks at **Grace**. *She remains silent.*

Grace   I don't –

Abeni   She receives it-o!

Pra   Put your faith in the Lord and He will not turn His back on you. He is here to help. Cast your burden on to Him. Let the Lord be the driver of your life. Take a seat and enjoy the ride.

Jovan   Vroom-vroom.

Abeni   That is right.

Pra   Someone is here with a burden. If you are ever laden, come out and let me pray for you.

Abeni (*to* **Grace**)   Why don't you go up?

She pushes **Grace** *to stand up.*

Grace   No, thank you.

Abeni   For your brother!

Grace   I said . . .

Jovan *gets up. They watch him walk over to* **Pastor Pra**. *He lays his hands on* **Jovan**'s *head and begins to pray for him.*

Abeni   You should have gone.

Grace   Why?

Abeni   Are you not here to seek help?

Grace   I don't know why I am here.

Abeni   Go there, let him pray for you. It will make you feel better.

Grace   Can he get Justice out? Will he perform a miracle?

Abeni   Only God can do that. But before He does you have to open your heart to Him.

Pra *finishes praying for* **Jovan***, who walks back to his seat. The service is over.* **Pra** *begins to walk out and the* **Congregation** *follows, singing and dancing as they exit.* **Grace** *follows behind, not inspired by the service.*

Congregation
We lift our hands in the sanctuary,
We lift our hands to give you the glory,
We lift our hands to give you the praise,
And we will praise you for the rest of our days! Yes!
We will praise you for the rest of our days!

Jesus! We give you the praise!
Emmanuel, we lift up your name!
Heavenly father! Coming Messiah!
And we will praise you for the rest of our days! Yes!
We will praise you for the rest of our days! Yes!

Scene Seven

Justice *is in the* **Guards***' kitchen at the detention centre. He has an apron on. There are various ingredients on the worktop. Two prison* **Guards** *are watching him as he chops some onions. He places a frying pan on a stove and he puts in some oil.*

Justice   Why are you two so quiet?

Guard 1   How long is this gonna take?

Guard 2   Yeah.

Justice   Food like this take time.

Guard 1   You don't have that long, mate.

Justice   You cannot rush greatness.

Guard 1   Greatness my arse. If you're caught in here we're all in trouble.

Justice   If a painter was painting, will you tell him to hurry up?

Guard 2   Is he painting my house?

Justice   An artist, not a house painter.

Guard 1   I'm not going to eat a painting, so get on with it.

Justice *puts the onions in the pan. He sprinkles some chilli powder and some pre-chopped red peppers and a pinch of salt. He is very at ease cooking.*

Guard 1   I don't want it too spicy.

Justice   This is an African dish. It needs to be spicy.

Guard 1 *gets up aggressively and* **Guard 2** *holds him back.*

Guard 1   I said I don't like it spicy.

Justice   Pepper is good for you.

Guard 2   He said he don't like it.

Justice   Calm down! Pepper – no pepper – not a problem. Relax, friends.

Guard 2   Who you telling to relax?

Justice   Hey, it was you that woke up in the middle of the night and asked me to cook you a meal.

Guard 1   You have been running your mouth for weeks about your special dish.

Justice   And your mouth was watering – you were dying to taste it.

Guard 2   Get on with it.

Justice   I will make it how you like it. This will be the best food you have ever tasted. You will be sending your women to me for me to teach them. When I get out of here I am going to apply to be on *MasterChef*. I will show this country how to make fantastic meals.

He adds four or five tomatoes and begins stirring.

Where is the meat?

Guard 1 *looks at* **Guard 2**.

Guard 2   What you looking at me for?

Guard 1   You have it!

Guard 2   You were meant to get it.

Guard 1   I got the vegetables.

Guard 2   Why would I get the meat?

Guard 1   That's what we decided.

Guard 2   When did we decide that?

Guard 1   When I said I will get the vegetables.

Guard 2   Where's the logic in that?

Justice   You didn't buy the meat?

Guard 2   It was his fault.

Guard 1   It's your fault.

Justice   You are both stupid!

Guards 1 *and* **2**   What?

They both get up out of their seats ready to pounce on **Justice**.

Justice   Don't worry, we can sort something out.

Guard 2   What you gonna do?

Justice *goes over to small fridge. He takes out some leftover beef in a Tupperware tub.*

Guard 1   You can't use that!

Justice *puts the meat under* **Guard 1**'s *nose. He pushes it away.*

Justice   Smell it.

He smells it.

It is fine.

He goes to pour the beef into a pan. He begins to stir it and cook it.

Guard 2   I am not eating that.

Justice   It is fine. I will cook it well. This will be the best stew you have ever eaten.

Guard 1   It's been in the fridge for ages.

Justice *turns up the heat.*

Justice   I will cook it well. The heat kill all the bacteria. It is only in this country that you get mad cow disease and it only because you do not cook your meat.

He goes to add some black pepper but catches **Guard 1**'s *eyes and stops. He then places the beef into the other pan with the onions and the tomatoes. He begins to stir the mixture. The* **Guards** *watch in silence.*

Scene Eight

A few weeks have passed.

Mr Cole *is at his desk. There are loads of books on immigration on the desk and littering the floor. There are also a few empty plastic coffee cups from Starbucks.* **Mr Cole** *looks tired. His shirt is unironed and his trousers are creased. He opens a can of Red Bull and begins drinking.*

Chi Chi *enters the room. She goes over to the fax machine and begins to send a fax.* **Mr Cole** *looks up from his desk.* **Chi Chi** *remains focused on sending the fax. Once it is sent she turns to leave, avoiding eye contact with* **Mr Cole**.

Mr Cole   Chi Chi.

Chi Chi *stops, but does not look at him.*

Chi Chi   Ever since you have been here, you have been snapping at me and I'm not having it any more.

Mr Cole   It's just –

Chi Chi   We all get stressed, it's no excuse.

Mr Cole   You are quite right.

Chi Chi   I am not a yo-yo.

Mr Cole   I know.

Chi Chi   All I was trying to do was be your friend. When you first came here I thought that it would finally be a chance for me to get the experience I need, working alongside a great lawyer. But you know what, I think you're strange. Everyone in this office thinks you are weird. Don't you notice I am the only one who bothers to talk to you?

Mr Cole   I am here to work, not make friends.

Chi Chi   See, that's the problem, because you act like this people don't trust you and in a place like this trust is everything. No one gets why you're here, and there are rumours going around that you're a spy.

Mr Cole (*begins to laugh*)   Spy?

Chi Chi   Yes, spy. You know that you are here to help spy on us for your buddies in the Home Office.

Mr Cole   I'm afraid I don't know anyone at the Home Office. If I did I would be pulling strings to get his appeal accepted.

Chi Chi   Yeah, right. You are a celebrity lawyer. I bet you and Boris are best of chums. You probably go to each other's houses and have dinner parties and all kinds of crap and meet up at MI5 to have strategic meetings and . . .

Mr Cole *begins to laugh.*

Chi Chi   I'm glad I amuse you.

Mr Cole   Can't you see how funny you are. Celebrity lawyer, that is hilarious.

Chi Chi   You just don't get it.

She turns to leave.

Mr Cole   Chi Chi, stop!

Chi Chi   Why are you here?

Mr Cole   I told you already.

Chi Chi   I'm not buying it.

Mr Cole   What do you want me to say?

Chi Chi   Just tell me the truth.

Mr Cole   I needed a change.

Chi Chi   You've been here almost a month and you've not settled in properly.

Mr Cole   I would disagree.

Chi Chi   You have a client in a detention centre. He must be going out of his mind, but you don't care. You sit at your desk all day long looking through books from morning to night. Do you even go home?

Mr Cole   Time is a sacrifice you make for a case.

Chi Chi   Sacrifice? What sacrifice? At the moment you don't do anything.

Mr Cole   I'm waiting to hear about the appeal.

Chi Chi   If you can't handle the case just say so. If you don't know how to deal with it, tell me, so I can find a lawyer who can.

Mr Cole   I don't need any assistance.

Chi Chi   Do something then. Stop waiting around, because if you're not careful, I told you already, they will fly him back. You have to go out and see your client. Make sure he's being treated well.

Mr Cole   I would appreciate it if you stopped telling me how to do my job!

Chi Chi   Well, get out there and do it then! This place needs a lawyer who is going to take control. If you thought you could just come here and chill in the office −

Mr Cole   I sit here reading because I have to know the facts, to get the evidence so I can help someone who needs my help. That is how I work. I do *not* win cases by going in blindly, I win them by being prepared!

He holds his head in pain. He goes to his drawer, takes out some tablets and goes to take them.

Did it ever occur to you that I never get a chance to do any work because you spend all day yapping?

Chi Chi   Pardon!

Mr Cole   I need to get on with the job, but you are like a bee buzzing in my ears all the time.

Chi Chi   I don't even know why I am bothering.

Mr Cole   I may not do things the way you expect. But I *do* win cases.

Chi Chi   Mr Cole, you may not notice it, you are wasting away. You don't look good. You want me to let you do your work. But since you been here, what have you achieved so far?

Mr Cole   How well you do your job as a lawyer is the only difference between innocent and guilty. I have never lost a case in my life.

Chi Chi   Whatever!

She goes to leave.

Mr Cole   Chi Chi, I want things to be cool with us.

Chi Chi   I can't be cool with someone I don't understand! The way you handled the Johnson case was amazing, but now . . .

Mr Cole   Working on the Johnson murder was one of the toughest cases I had to deal with, and I don't intend to make the same mistake I made with that case.

Chi Chi   What mistakes?

Mr Cole   It doesn't matter.

Chi Chi   Tell me.

Mr Cole   No.

Chi Chi   See what I am saying about you – so secretive.

Mr Cole   It didn't occur to me till it was too late that Dwayne White was innocent and by that time I couldn't do anything. I couldn't stop the case.

Chi Chi   You knew he was innocent?

Mr Cole   My job as a prosecutor is to present the evidence, and although I am here to defend Justice, I still need to gather evidence.

Chi Chi   He committed suicide! He took his own life because he was convicted of a murder he did not commit and you knew he was innocent?

Mr Cole   How is that the only thing you took from what I just told you?

Chi Chi   I've defended you to everyone I know and you knew he was –

Mr Cole   When it was too late!

Chi Chi   He was innocent!

Mr Cole   Him being innocent is not the point of the conversation.

Chi Chi   I can't believe what I am hearing. To me it is!

Mr Cole   You live in a fantasy world.

Chi Chi   Yeah, if that is the world people do the right thing.

Mr Cole   Do you honestly think law is such a walk in the fucking park?

Chi Chi   You sent an innocent guy to prison . . .

Mr Cole   The jury convicted him. They came up with the verdict. I presented the evidence. For a law student you are absolutely clueless. You don't pay attention to the right things.

Chi Chi   I can't believe this.

Mr Cole   I can't believe you. We do not live in a simple world. It is not black or white. It is ninety per cent white, and in order to survive you and I have to be better than the best. That is what each case is about. You look at me and don't get why I am in early and leave late. If you want to survive in this world, the world of law, you have to. Otherwise you will never get noticed. *Ever!* So when I have the chance to win a case, I do just that! I work hard to *win*. You have to win regardless of the fucking case, because if you lose *you lose everything*, and I have worked all my life for –

Chi Chi   What? Injustice and lies? I don't think you're in the right mind frame to do this job.

Mr Cole   Do you ever listen?

Chi Chi   I heard you loud and clear. It is not about the people you help. It is about yourself and your ego. That is not why I am here, why I am going into law.

Mr Cole   What experiences have you had? You think you have all the answers but you haven't even figured out that in life there are more questions than answers. You have to live to understand the world.

Chi Chi   I know right from wrong.

Mr Cole   You are just a kid, Chi Chi, what would you know?

Chi Chi   A kid? Whatever makes you sleep at night?

Scene Nine

Back at the detention centre. **Justice** *is being chased by the two* **Guards**. *They corner him.*

Justice   Please, I didn't do it.

Guard 1   You tried to kill us!

Justice   It was not my fault!

Guard 2   You gave me food poisoning.

Justice   I didn't know.

Guard 1   You thought you were funny.

Justice   Believe me, I thought it was alright to eat. I ate it too. You saw me.

Guard 2   Why didn't you get sick?

Justice   I don't know.

Guard 1 *has a can of dog food with a spoon in it.* **Justice** *scurries into a corner.*

Justice   Why are you doing this?

Guard 1   Eat it!

Justice   Please, I can't!

Guard 2   He said eat it.

Justice *opens his mouth and* **Guard 1** *feeds him the dog food.*

Guard 1   Swallow it!

Justice   I . . .

Guard 2 *grabs* **Justice** *by the mouth. He forces him to swallow it.* **Justice** *tries to resist but is forced.*

Guard 2   Open wide.

Guard 1 *takes another scoop and* **Justice** *tries to fight it. The* **Guards** *hold him down and force the food down his throat.*

Guard 1   This is going to be your food until you go back to the jungle.

Guard 2   You better get used to the taste.

Guard 1   Yeah, that's right.

Justice   Please stop it.

Scene Ten

It is 5 p.m. **Grace** *is outside the Home Office. She is pacing up and down, waiting for* **Alfred** *to leave. She runs up to him waving a paper in his face.*

Grace   Excuse me!

Alfred   You again?

Grace   Why did you reject his appeal?

Alfred   If you don't stop harassing me, I will call the police.

Grace   Why are you doing this to him?

Alfred   What happens to him is nothing to do with me,

Grace   You are the caseworker, I know you are the one doing this. You locked him in a place he does not deserve to be in.

Alfred *tries to go but she stands in his way.*

Alfred   Stalking is an offence.

Grace *continues to block* **Alfred***'s way.*

Grace   I need to get him out of the detention centre. He called me and they are not treating him well. Why are you being like this?

Alfred   Your brother broke the law.

Grace   Is there nothing you can do to help him? What has Justice done to you? If this was the other way round, Justice would be merciful to you.

Alfred   I am not an immigrant.

Grace   Why are you punishing him?

Alfred   I don't make the rules!

Grace   But you are enforcing them! Please, look into your heart and find compassion for my brother. He is a good person. Your rules are unfair.

Alfred   Everyone has to follow them. Your brother is not above the law. None of you people are. You can't just come here and do what you want. He should have not entered the country illegally. Where he is now and how he ends up is all his own doing.

Grace   He cannot go back to Zimbabwe. There are so many other immigrants that are here that should not be, criminals that are here to make trouble. My brother is only here to seek refuge.

Alfred   He should have done so by the proper method.

Grace   Why can't you understand?

Alfred   What is there for me to understand? This country is overcrowded as it is. You cannot just come here and want to get a piece of the pie when you have done nothing to deserve it.

Grace   If our country was in a better state we would not be here.

Alfred   For the last time, get out of my way!

Grace   How can you condemn your own? You turn your back on people who need help. We are not animals. They use you to choose the fate of your own and you do not see the problem with that.

Alfred   I am British.

Grace   Are you not black? You see your own people suffering and you do nothing to help.

Alfred   Yes! Cos that is my job. Sorting out countries that are ruled by useless leaders. And what role do you play in it exactly? You think this country is a pushover. That's what you all believe.

Grace   It is only the luck of the draw that you are here. Your family were once foreigner in this land.

Alfred   Unlike you and *your* people, my family did not smuggle themselves in a truck to get here. They walked proudly through the borders. They were British citizens from birth. They had the right to enter, work and settle here. They were invited to this country.

Grace   And what were they invited here to do? Was it not to work in jobs that the immigrants you hate so much do right now?! The invitation was not limited to *your* people. My father was invited to this country to work in 'your' hospitals. But instead of being a follower and going in search of a better world, he had hope our country will get better. He did not want to be a slave in another man's land. He was loyal to his own land.

Alfred   Your father was a fool.

Grace   My father was a man! A man of honour and courage. He like many other Zimbabweans were willing to work hard to create a better future for our country. He struggled for the piece of land that –

Alfred   Save it for someone who cares.

He begins to walk off but **Grace** *holds on to him.*

Grace   It is not your fault. Ignorance is the curse of our race.

Alfred   Get out of my way.

Grace   You look down on me like I am so different to you. We are all immigrants in this land! You should not be so blind to the truth!

He pushes her away and she falls back. **Ben** *comes out of the office and runs to her aid.*

Ben   Oi. What is happening here?

Alfred   I'm glad you're here to witness this. This is the woman that has been bugging me all week.

Grace (*to* **Ben**)   I am just trying to make him see that my brother needs to be set free.

Ben   Come inside, babes.

Alfred   Why are you taking her inside?

Ben   She is upset, man. (*To* **Grace**.) Don't worry, beautiful. Tell me the problem. I can help, babes.

Scene Eleven

Grace *is in the detention centre waiting to see* **Justice**. *She has been crying and her eyes are red.* **Justice** *is brought in by a* **Guard**. *He takes a seat, his head lowered. They both sit in silence for a while.*

Grace   I am working double shift to raise the money for your ticket.

Justice *remains silent.*

Grace   That is the only way to get you out of here, Justice.

Justice *does not look up.*

Grace   This country is no good.

Justice *does not respond.*

Grace   You will be better off back home.

Silence.

What do you want me to do?

Justice *remains silent.*

Grace   Justice?

He looks up.

Did you hear what I said?

Justice *remains silent.*

Grace   JUSTICE!

Justice   I want to get out.

Grace   I tried to help but . . . the case officer will not change his mind about the appeal.

Justice   I don't like it in here.

Grace   That is why we need to get you back home.

Justice   I don't want to go back home. I want to stay in this country.

Grace   They don't want you here.

Justice   I can't go back! If I go they will . . .

Grace   Zimbabwe has changed.

Justice   How do you know?

Grace   It has . . . it . . . it has to.

Justice   Mugabe is still in control.

Grace   Morgan has a say now. MDC have a fifty-fifty power share.

Justice   Don't be so stupid. Who controls the army, the police? You are talking like a foreigner. The power share is nothing but a mask. Nothing has changed. Putting a plaster on a wound is not what makes it heal.

Grace   Justice, I don't know what else to do to help you. All I know is if I raise the money for your ticket, they will release you.

Justice   ZANU-PF still have a stronghold. If I go back do you think they will not look for me? Everyone in town knows my views, where I stand, what I think of ZANU-PF. I was a member of the anti-corruption team that was set up to address all violence used for political reasons. You tell me, sista, you believe that the minute I land that I would not be shot or hanged?

Grace   Do you want to rot and die in here? Because I tried everything to get you out. I even went to church to look for help. At least back home you will be free.

Justice   You want me to go back when those that have killed my friend, threatened my life, are still walking around. I want to live in a place where I can have a future.

Grace   There is no future for you in this place.

Justice There is no economy in Zimbabwe. There are no jobs, no money. If you go to the hospitals there are no medicines, no doctors. because they are not getting paid. Go to school, there are no teachers, because they are not getting paid. There is no future there either!

Grace You still care for our people. Maybe you can help change things.

Justice You are not listening to me.

Grace You are not listening to me.

Justice The first chance you got you ran far away.

Grace I did not run. How can you say that?

Justice You only care about yourself. You had no reason to escape. You were not hunted. You never put yourself forward for anything. You remained silent all your life. My friend used to tell me what a useless sister I have.

Grace *slaps him and he slaps her back.*

Justice You run to this country and you use my life, my story, my struggle to get your stay, to come here and seek asylum, *and you come here and tell me I should go back*! You came to this country and you became me! When I am the one who suffered! What makes you better than me? How can you think that it is OK for you to do such a thing?

Grace I didn't –

Justice WHAT?! WHAT?! What didn't you think?! That I wanted out too?

Grace You love Zimbabwe more than I do.

Justice I LOVE MY LIFE MORE. I would rather remain here for the rest of my life, caged like an animal, than to be set free there. If this was the other way around would I not do all I can to save you? I would give my life for you. Don't you think you owe me more than your life?

Silence.

I asked you a question, Grace.

Grace   I am trying to do the best I can! I have not eaten, not slept. All because I want to . . .

She begins to cry.

Justice   I have noticed since you have been here your ability to shed a tear is award-winning. Have you been practising? Is that what you were taught? To have a convincing story you need to know how to cry. Is that why they believe you and not me, because you can switch on those tears like a tap?

Grace *stops crying immediately.*

Grace   IT IS NOT MY FAULT YOU ARE IN THIS SITUATION!

Justice   YES IT IS. It is your fault. They think I am a liar when it is you that stole my freedom. YOU TOOK MY LIFE.

Grace   What do you want me to do?

Justice   Do whatever it takes to get me out of here ! My life is in your hands. I am your flesh and blood.

Scene Twelve

Pra, Jovan, Abeni *and* **Grace** *are out to lunch all dressed up in their traditional attire. They have just finished church and are in an African restaurant, eating. The table is covered with food. Monica fish, plantain and rice.*

Jovan *is struggling to eat the food. He keeps taking a sip of water and cooling his mouth, while the others eat the food with ease.*

Abeni   God is good.

Pra   He is fantastic.

Jovan   Pastor Pra, today service was very inspiring.

Pra   Thank you!

Abeni   Don't give him a big head.

Jovan   The congregation is getting bigger and bigger.

Pra   The Lord is bringing them in.

Abeni   Grace, you are very quiet.

Pra   You should feel good after the service.

She nods, unconvinced.

Unless you feel I didn't do a good job.

Abeni   Ahh, you did a good job. The spirit of the Lord is alive today.

Jovan (*to* **Grace**)   Something is on your mind. Problem shared is a problem halved.

Abeni   Are you worried about Justice?

Jovan   How is he doing?

Pra   Did you not hear the service today, people? (*To* **Grace**.) Have faith, my sister. It will all work out in the end.

Abeni   Keep preaching!

Pra   God will guide Justice out of his problem.

Jovan   He has a plan.

Pra   And He gives us what we need.

Abeni   We thank God for providing us with good health.

Jovan   We may not have that red book but we have freedom –

Abeni   – and we pray for that more than we pray for anything else.

Pra   Amen!

Abeni   It is all about believing.

Grace   In what?

Abeni   In God!

Grace   Justice is stuck in a detention centre and –

Pra   – you blame God.

Grace   Yes, I do.

Abeni   Ahh, please God, forgive her-o. It is the devil talking.

She goes into her bag and begins to sprinkle holy water all around.

Grace   I do not want His forgiveness.

Pra   You don't mean that!

Grace   Yes, I do.

Jovan   We have all at one point feel how you feel.

Abeni   Yes-o. I used to think all the time and say to people, He has not done anything for me.

Pra   But He gave you the precious gift of all. He gave you life.

Jovan   When people used to say that to me, I would say I didn't ask for it. I would shout at my friends and say, your God is a lazy God. He wants me to be thankful or grateful for what? He created the world, is He not responsible for it?

Abeni   Life is hard-o. Very hard!

Pra   But it harder without faith.

Jovan   Or hope.

Abeni   Leave it in God's hand.

Pra   He will sort it out.

Abeni   Come, let us pray.

Grace *shakes her head.*

Pra   You need to pray for strength.

Jovan   Yes. I think she needs that right now. You are so much like me, Grace, when I first started coming to church.

Pra   You always asked question. You used to ask if God was a man or a woman. Is He black or white?

Abeni   It is irrelevant, all that matter is He is a loving God.

Pra   Correct.

Abeni   Many people have doubt, Grace. You are not the only one. At one stage in our lives we will ask many questions because we doubt our faith. Why is the world full of evil? God knows everything, but yet He does not prevent bad things from happening. How can He not know what type of world He would be creating?

Jovan   That is the thing that people forget. He gave us free will.

Grace   The same free will He gave the man that is using you, abusing the fact that he has your life in his hand because you have his name.

Jovan   It is different.

Grace   It is all the same. You of all people should understand where I am coming from. How long have you been praying for your so-called God to sort out your problem, and is it anywhere near sorted? You are trapped in a predicament you cannot get yourself out of. Do you not ask yourself who put you in it? You should be mad with God for allowing you to be in this situation. If there is a God, I am mad at Him.

Abeni   This is what the devil does-o. He makes us doubt the Lord. The devil is a liar! The devil is a liar!

Pra   Justice will be out in no time. Just believe.

Abeni   There has to be a God. We have to believe someone or something is looking out for us. Otherwise what is the point of going on? Faith is believing when you don't see. Or understand.

Pra   Put all your questions into your prayers. The reason people are suffering is because the world we live in is evil. The world is under God's curse because of man's rebellion against God's word. We are all born with sin. But He has promised to set things right. 'God shall wipe away all tears from their eyes and there shall be no death, neither sorrow, nor crying, neither shall there be any pain.'

Jovan   Revelation 21:4.

Pra   You are stronger than you think. He would not put you through this if He thought you could not handle it.

Abeni   God uses situations in our lives to test us.

Jovan   To teach us faith and patience.

Grace   You rely too much on faith. I believe in reality. If I waited for your so-called God to help me, I would be stuck in Zimbabwe. I made my path, I created my own destiny. So stop telling me all the time to have this stupid thing called faith.

Pra   Our destiny is already decided. Justice will be out. It is down to you to believe it and open your arms to receive it. Without faith it is impossible to please Him, for he who comes to God must believe that He is, and that He is a rewarder of those who diligently seek him.

Jovan   Hebrews 11:6.

Grace   *You don't understand.* I am not like you people. I cannot sit and wait for an invisible force to save me. I save myself. I will be the one to get my brother out of there.

Pra   It is not your battle. It is God's battle. No man on earth can do His job.

Scene Thirteen

Chi Chi *is at her desk in the office.* **Mr Cole** *enters, smartly dressed. He runs over to his desk and goes through his paperwork.*

Chi Chi   I thought you left.

Mr Cole   You thought wrong.

Chi Chi   I have been looking for the files for Justice Ncube.

Mr Cole   I am still dealing with his case.

Chi Chi   You need to hand them to me.

Mr Cole I said I am dealing with it! I have got him a date for the AIT.

Chi Chi You got what? No one gets a date that quick. How did you do it? Well done. When is it? This is exciting!

Mr Cole (*continuing to search on his desk*) Do you have his sister's number?

Chi Chi You had the file last.

Mr Cole I can't find it. Where the heck is this thing?

He drops all the paper on his table. **Chi Chi** *goes over to help him.*

Chi Chi She is going to be really pleased. Haven't seen her about recently.

Mr Cole Where is this damn number?

Chi Chi Have you told Justice the news?

Mr Cole I wanted to get a date first.

Chi Chi Where did you put it last?

Mr Cole I wouldn't be looking for it if I knew that. Can you help me look for her number?

They begin to look around on the table for **Grace***'s number.*

Mr Cole I wish I had more power.

Chi Chi Power is not always a good thing. Remember the story you told me? The real *Lord of the Rings* or something . . . Ring of Gyges.

Mr Cole What about it?

Chi Chi The guy finds a ring on a dead giant in a tomb. He takes the ring and finds out that the ring gives him invisibility power when he presses a button. He uses this power to seduce the wife of the King, and with her help he murders the King so he can become King and be in charge. That the story, right?

Mr Cole Yes.

Chi Chi   So I am right!

Mr Cole   About what?

Chi Chi   Power corrupts and absolute power corrupts abso –
even more. Do you want to have that responsibility?

Mr Cole   When I told you the story it was not about power
corrupting. You thought *The Lord of the Rings* was original. I
just wanted to show you it wasn't.

Chi Chi   *And I am showing you the story had a meaning.* Stop
trying to go off track. This guy who had the ring can represent
any and anyone. He could be Joe Bloggs, geeky and weak, but
the minute he has power he will use it to his advantage and in
most cases that advantage is for bad even if he did originally
have good intentions. People with power always abuse it.

Mr Cole   Power on its own can do no harm . . . It was not
the ring that was dishonest. It was the person who used it.

Chi Chi   Power does not stand alone. For it to be of any
use, we have to interact with it. Power is not what you need.
It's understanding. You may not win this case with Justice, you
got to prepare yourself for that. You have to put presenting
the truth above everything else. I may be young, Mr Cole,
and see the world in a more colourful light than you, but it's
because I want to make it better. If everyone that goes into
this practice has the same objective then I believe that people
like Justice will be judged fairly. You got to aim to do the right
thing, that is what the world needs. You may say it's just a
fantasy and it's not going to come true, but what is the harm
in trying?

Mr Cole   I would love to live on your planet. I wish you the
best luck in the world.

Chi Chi   Negative comments like that are not going to faze
me. As they say in *Bugsy Malone*, 'You give a little love and it
all comes back to you, la la la la la la la. You know you're
gonna be remembered for the thing that you say and do, la la
la . . . '

Mr Cole *laughs.*

Chi Chi   See, I am spreading a bit of happiness your way.

Mr Cole   I am laughing because you can't sing.

Chi Chi   For your information, I have been told by many people that I have a voice of a mermaid.

Mr Cole   You mean a banshee!

Chi Chi   That's not very nice.

Mr Cole   Got to keep it real with you, my dear!

Chi Chi   I don't care what you say. I can sing. Listen. 'When a hero comes along – '

Mr Cole   Stop . . .

He covers his ears. **Chi Chi** *goes round him and begins to sing in his ears.*

Chi Chi   ' – Strength to carry on, you can cast your fears aside and you know you can survive and when you feel like hope is gone – '

Mr Cole   Enough! You're meant to be helping me find this file. His sister needs to know about his appeal hearing. I need to let her know she can relax.

Scene Fourteen

Ben *and* **Grace** *are in a bedroom, half naked.* **Grace** *gets up and begins to get dressed.* **Ben** *tries to kiss her again.*

Ben   Come on, baby, where are you going?

Grace   What day will my brother be released?

Ben   You smell so nice, come on . . .

He goes to kiss her on the lips. She moves her face. He stops.

What is wrong with you?

Grace   My brother . . .

Ben   You talk about him too much!

Grace   When are you going to release him?

Ben   Excuse me?

Grace   You got what you want. Now you can return the favour.

Ben   Oh my days, are you trying to play me? Is that why you called me . . . asked me to meet you? How could I not see this? You are good!

Grace   My brother needs to be out by tomorrow.

Ben (*begins to laugh*)   Tomorrow? Who did you think I was, the Home Secretary or something?

He gets out of the bed and begins to put on his clothes.

I got no control over what happens in detention centres. I'm only an enforcement officer.

Grace   You promised to help.

Ben   Yeah, to make you feel good, take your mind off it. Help you relax.

He continues to laugh.

Grace   You said . . . I am going to call the police and . . .

She goes for her bag and takes out her phone. He takes it from her.

Ben   I should call the police on you. You tried to blackmail me. Entrapment is not legal. You are one crazy lady, you know that!

He begins to put his clothes on quickly.

You women are dangerous creatures. I am a married man. I don't have time for this. Tryna run game on me.

Grace   Please, you are the only one that can help.

Ben   I can't help you.

Grace   Please, no . . . don't do this . . .

Ben   Babes, you got our wires crossed, love.

Grace   I will do anything.

She tries to take his clothes off but he brushes her off.

Ben   No, thanks. You weren't even all that!

Scene Fifteen

That evening.

Abeni, **Jovan** and **Pra** *are all on a station platform waiting for a train to arrive. As it pulls up at the station, passengers exit, dropping litter and newspapers as they go.* **Pra**, **Jovan** and **Abeni** *go to opposite sides of the train to pick up the rubbish left behind.*

Pra   Has Grace called you, Abeni?

Abeni   No.

Jovan   I hope she is alright.

Abeni   These people are filthy. Look at all de rubbish I have to pick up.

A **Passer-by** *walks across* **Abeni** *and drops a packet of crisps and a carton of drink. The drink spills on the floor.* **Abeni** *calls her back.*

Abeni   Excuse me!

Passer-by *ignores her and keeps walking.*

Abeni   EXCUSE ME!

Jovan *notices* **Abeni** *calling the* **Passer-by** *and taps her on the shoulder. She takes out her headset.*

Jovan   The lady over there is calling you.

Passer-by *(turns round)*   Yes?

Abeni   You dropped this.

She points to the litter.

Passer-by Yeah.

Abeni And it is on the floor.

Passer-by Yes.

Jovan What she is say is, you need to go back and pick up rubbish.

Passer-by Why?

Jovan Because you fall it.

Passer-by I don't have time for this.

Abeni Where are you going? This rubbish is not going to pick itself.

*The **Passer-by** begins to walk off, but is stopped by **Jovan**.*

Jovan Hey!

Passer-by What do you want?

Jovan You fall rubbish, go and pick it up.

Pra *joins in.*

Pra That is right!

Passer-by I am not picking it up.

Pra Why?

Passer-by There is three of you, it is not a difficult job. English may not be your first language but simple maths should be universal.

*She tries to walk off but **Pra** stands in her way.*

Passer-by Get out of the way.

Abeni We are not your slave.

Passer-by You are a cleaner, your job – as it states in the first part of the word – is to *clean*.

Pra Yes, the trains.

Jovan   Not to pick up after lazy people.

Passer-by   I would watch your mouth if I was you.

She moves real close to **Jovan**, *who moves in closer.*

Pra   Jovan, leave it!

Jovan   No. (*To* **Passer-by**.) Pick up your mess.

Passer-by   Would you like me to speak to your manager?

Pra   My friend, you don't need to do that. We are apologetic.

Abeni   Jovan, let's leave it!

Jovan   No, I am not afraid.

He takes out his phone.

Call him. I have my papers.

Silence.

Passer-by   I have better things to do with my time.

Jovan   Go back over there and pick it up.

Abeni   Jovan, it is OK. I will do it.

She goes over and picks up the carton, then gets down on her knees to wipe the spilled drink.

Passer-by   She is the smart one.

Pra   You are very rude person!

The **Passer-by** *pushes past* **Pra** *and* **Jovan** *and walks off.*

Jovan (*to* **Abeni**)   Why did you do that?

Abeni   It is not worth it.

Jovan   I don't care.

Pra   Why did you say you had your papers?

Jovan   Because they take piss when they think you don't have.

Pra   You are playing a dangerous game.

He pushes **Jovan**.

Jovan   We have to correct people when they behave incorrectly.

Abeni   Pra is right. Have you forgotten your name is not Jovan, and God forbid if they look at your papers properly. Some fights are just not worth fighting.

Pra   She is right.

Jovan *and* **Pra** *goes over to help* **Abeni**.

Jovan   You are both wrong. This is why these people get away with it.

Abeni   It is OK.

Jovan   It is not.

Pra   What do you think would have happened if she really called the manager?

Abeni   We would have got fired!

Jovan   Not true, he is a nice man –

Pra   – who does not want any problems. The government is not just making it hard for us, they are making it hard for people to *hire* us. Do you think he wants to risk getting fined?

Abeni   You know how many people have come and gone in this job?

Pra   He will not think twice to get rid of us if he thinks we are causing problems.

Jovan   We have rights, you know.

Abeni   That is the thing, Jovan – we do not. Do not fool yourself.

Jovan   How can you say that? We are human being.

Pra   *With the wrong papers!*

Jovan   It doesn't mean we should be treated any different.

Abeni   You want to put pride above freedom. Do that-o. But I am warning you, you will regret it and I don't want any part of it.

Jovan   These people in this country forget, if they did not have us this country will fall to pieces. We are doing job none of them want. They would rather go on benefit and sit down all day long not working than to clean and they want to complain when I am ready to do this job.

Pra   We know that! You are preaching to the choir.

Jovan   I find that very degrading, having to rely on people to pay your way.

Pra   We agree!

Jovan   They should treat us fair!

Abeni   *We know!*

Pra   You need to remember you are here to work to support your family back home. Don't mind people like that. Don't let the devil win.

Abeni   He has been testing all of us.

Pra   Let us pray!

The group holds hands. Two **Passengers** *walk past them and look on with disapproving gazes.*

Dear Lord, you are our light and our salvation. You are the stronghold in our lives – of whom shall we be afraid? When evil men advance against us to devour our flesh, when enemies and foes attack us, they will stumble and fall.

Abeni   Amen.

Jovan   Amen.

Pra   Our hearts will not fear, even when war breaks out around us, even then will we be more confident. Give us strength, Lord, to go on. Amen.

Jovan *and* **Abeni**   Amen.

Pra   Do you feel better?

Jovan *nods.*

An announcement comes over the PA system.

Announcer   The train at Platform 5 is ready to board.

Abeni *links arms with* **Jovan** *and* **Pra**.

Abeni   Come on, let's go.

Two **Passengers** *walk past the three and make a comment.*

Passenger 1   Look at them, you would think they don't have work to do.

Passenger 2   For real. They must love this job . . . easy.

Jovan *turns to resspond.* **Pra** *and* **Abeni** *drag him along as they continue walking.*

Jovan   Excu –

Pra   It is not worth it, my broda.

Abeni   He is right, let's go to lunch.

Passengers fill the platform and drown out the three.

Scene Sixteen

Later on in the afternoon.

Mr Cole *is sitting at a table. He is dressed smartly and his face looks fresh. He is waiting for* **Justice** *to arrive.* **Justice** *is followed into the room with a* **Guard**. *He sits down at the table, avoiding eye contact. He looks drained and withdrawn.*

Mr Cole   Hello, Justice.

Justice *remains silent.*

Mr Cole   It's a pleasure to finally meet you.

He puts out his hand for a handshake. **Justice** *ignores him.*

Mr Cole   My name is Mr Cole. I have been appointed to your case.

Justice *looks down at his hand.*

Mr Cole   We are really excited that we got another appeal hearing. It is good news.

Justice *does not look up.*

Mr Cole   I can see that you want to get out of here.

Silence.

Justice   Nobody cares.

Mr Cole   Justice, listen to me, I care. That is why I am here. I am here to help you

A tear drops from **Justice**'s *eyes.*

Justice   When can I leave?

Mr Cole   Not yet. I put in an application for bail and unfortunately it was rejected, but –

Justice *gets up to leave.* **Mr Cole** *rises to stop him.* **Justice** *begins to cry.* **Mr Cole** *stands looking uncomfortable. He searches his pocket for a tissue.*

Justice   Why are they treating me like a criminal?

Mr Cole *turns to the* **Guard** *in the corner.*

Mr Cole (*to the* **Guard**)   Do you have a tissue?

The **Guard** *shrugs.*

Mr Cole   CAN YOU GO GET THE MAN A TISSUE?!

The **Guard** *reluctantly gets up.* **Mr Cole** *goes over to* **Justice**. *He tries to get eye contact with him.*

Mr Cole   Justice, look at me.

Justice *looks away.*

Mr Cole   Please look at me.

Justice *raises his head slightly.*

Mr Cole   I am doing everything I can to get you out of here. I am sorry I did not come and see you sooner.

Justice   I did not commit a murder or steal from anyone.

Mr Cole (*goes to hug him*)   Hang in there, Justice.

Justice *begins sobbing uncontrollably. His cries get louder and louder.*

Justice   I just want to get out. I don't want to stay here any more.

Mr Cole (*hugs him tighter*)   Hang in there.

Justice   Please help me to get out of here.

He continues to sob. The **Guard** *returns.*

Mr Cole (*to the* **Guard**)   Has he had a medical assessment?

Guard *shrugs.*

Mr Cole   This is unacceptable.

Guard   You're going to have to speak to my manager –

Mr Cole   It's obvious he's no fit state to still be detained.

Guard   It's not up to me what –

Mr Cole   Can't you see his health is deteriorating?

Guard   I'm just here to –

Mr Cole   Are you not aware of his health needs?

Guard   My job is to –

Mr Cole   Your job is to look after his well-being. I want to see a copy of his medical notes.

Guard   I don't have access to –

Mr Cole   Useless.

Guard   Excuse me. You can't just come in here and insult me.

Mr Cole   I want to see the referral form that your team has sent to the Medical Foundation for the Care of Victims of Torture.

Guard   I'm not trying to be difficult, but you will need to put that request in writing.

Mr Cole   I'm making a verbal request.

Guard   I'm afraid we don't accept that. Now if you'll excuse me −

Mr Cole   It is very clear that you are not doing your job properly.

Guard   I don't appreciate your tone or −

Mr Cole   And I don't appreciate a client being detained inappropriately. It is in your directorate operational guidelines that detention is considered unsuitable, in exceptional circumstances, for those suffering from serious medical conditions or mental illness. He is in no fit state to be here. Why is he still being detained?

Guard   I do not −

Mr Cole   I'll wait right here till you get back to me with a better answer.

Guard   Who do you think you are, coming in here telling me how to do my job?

Mr Cole   If you knew how to do it in the first place, I wouldn't have to tell you.

Guard   You can't talk to me like that. I'm going to report you.

Mr Cole   If I were you, I would be looking for a new job.

Guard   Are you threatening me?

Mr Cole   I am merely giving you a heads-up. This place is a sham and when I'm done with my report you may not have a job to come back to

Guard *laughs.*

Mr Cole I'm glad you find it funny.

Guard I find *you* funny. Who do you think you are? This government puts immigration at the top of their list. It has for the last few years, and one guideline that I do remember that is constantly drummed down my throat is, it is the norm that those with failed asylum claims will be detained. The rules are set. Now you can judge me all you like and you can go around strutting your stuff and acting like you are better than me. But detention centres are here to stay whether you like it or not. As long as the government feels that establishment such as this helps strengthen their border controls. No amount of noise from you or me will change that. (*To* **Justice**.) Justice, let's go.

The **Guard** *goes up to* **Justice**, *helps him to his feet and takes him out.*

Mr Cole He is not going anywhere with you. This man is not stepping a foot back into a cell. Believe me!

Scene Seventeen

We are in an African restaurant. **Justice** *is out of the detention centre.* **Grace** *is sitting silently.* **Jovan**, **Pra** *and* **Abeni** *are tucking in to their food.*

Pra Praise the Lord!

Abeni, **Jovan** *and* **Justice** Hallelujah!

Pra I SAID PRAISE THE LORD.

Abeni, **Jovan** *and* **Justice** HALLELUJAH.

Abeni begins to sing and the rest join in.

Abeni
We are saying thank you, Jesus.

Pra *and* **Jovan**
Thank you, my Lord.

All
> We are saying thank you, Jesus.
> Thank you, my Lord.

Pra   I told you to have faith. God always delivers.

Grace   It is not over yet! He has only been granted temporary leave to remain. You are still going to have to continue this process and –

Justice   You don't have to worry about me. I am going to Italy tomorrow.

Grace   Italy? You cannot travel.

Justice   You said it yourself, there is still a chance of me getting sent back. I am not going there.

Grace   What is wrong with you?

Justice   I will be OK.

Jovan *jumps out of his seat unexpectedly.*

Jovan   I am coming too!

Pra *and* **Abeni**   What!

Grace   Justice, you are not going to Italy.

Abeni   You too, Jovan!

Jovan   Why? I don't like this country. I am killing myself and for what?

Justice   This country does not like us.

Pra   Italy is no different to this place. You are going to face the same problem there that you do here.

Justice   And if I do, I will go to Germany.

Jovan   Or we can go to France.

Justice   We will go anywhere!

Grace   You plan to spend your life running?

Justice   I want to be free.

Jovan   I need a new start. You should all come along. Let us do it together.

Abeni   I am staying here and so are you.

Jovan   I am going.

Justice   I plan to get a ticket tomorrow. (*To* **Pra**.) Can one of your friends prepare my papers?

Grace   You are very selfish.

Justice   Yes, because I have to be! What did you do to help me?

Abeni   Ahh. You better say sorry to your sister, she has been running –

Grace   Do you not worry, Abeni. (*To* **Justice**.) You are a man now. Your life is your own.

Pra   I think you both have to think about this.

Grace   Leave them.

Abeni   How can you say that? We can't let them go. Pra, say something.

Jovan   Nothing is going to make me change my mind. I need a new start.

Justice *hugs* **Jovan**. **Grace** *gets up to leave.*

Abeni   Grace, wait.

Grace   I have to make up the hours I missed at work. (*To* **Justice**.) You have my number, call me when you arrive there.

Justice *goes to give his sister a big hug*

Justice   I love you, sister.

Grace   Have a safe journey.

Abeni   What are you people talking? It is not a good idea. Pra, say something. Why are you silent? Tell them.

Pra   May the Lord continue to be your guide on your journey.

Jovan   Italy, here we come!

Scene Eighteen

Mr Cole *is back in the office. He is putting all his books into a box and emptying out the office.* **Chi Chi** *enters.*

Chi Chi   Congratulations, Mr Cole. You did a great job. This is the first time we ever got a result like that. I knew you could do it. What you doing?

Mr Cole *ignores* **Chi Chi** *and continues to pack.*

Chi Chi   Why are you packing?

Mr Cole   This is it for me.

Chi Chi   We did what you set out to do. We won! I know I've been a pain in the arse, but I let fear get the better –

Mr Cole   I'm not suited for this job.

Chi Chi   You are!

Mr Cole   I'm just not that guy.

Chi Chi   What guy? What are you on about?

Mr Cole   The type of person who should be doing a job like this.

Chi Chi   What is wrong? Talk to me. You're not being fair on yourself.

Mr Cole   I'm not being *harsh* enough on myself.

Chi Chi   What are you on about?

Mr Cole   I am not in the position to fight for someone, rights when I am not a *just* man.

Chi Chi   A just man is no different from an unjust man. *You taught me that!* We are all the same. We learn to be good, no man is born good and pure. We learn from experience. *This is an experience*. Don't you get it? You care – a man who cares is more good than bad. He can do more good.

Mr Cole   Injustice pays better than the truth in this world.

Chi Chi   It doesn't, or else you wouldn't be feeling guilty about the Johnson case. Is this not what it's all about? Give it time.

Mr Cole   When you make a mistake, you can't go back.

Chi Chi   No. So keep moving forward. Our job is to challenge the law. We can do this . . . we can change the laws, it's possible.

Mr Cole   I didn't come here to change the law.

Chi Chi   You can't go, Mr Cole. We need you here. I know you like to take your time and it's something I will have to get used to. I don't mind getting used to it. I'll learn to keep my mouth shut, I promise.

Mr Cole   Since I've been here, I have made no difference to the work you do.

Chi Chi   Yes, you have! Justice is out.

Mr Cole   I only got him 'temporary leave to remain'. He still has another battle.

Chi Chi   Yes, but as you said at the appeal hearing, Justice had always maintained contact with the Immigration Service prior to being detained. He had no reason to be detained in the first place. They have to grant him his stay.

Mr Cole   The world we live in . . . it's not a fair one.

Chi Chi   Tell me something new! Is that not why we're here? You are your own worst enemy. We need you! Stop making me beg.

Mr Cole   These people we want to help are never going to find fairness in the law. The system is set up for them to lose.

Chi Chi   Stop having a blanket view. Every case is different.

Mr Cole   But the rules remain the same, and what the government classes as right may never bring justice to the people we want to help.

Chi Chi   It can't stop us from trying. This is just your first case and you set Justice free.

Mr Cole *ignores* **Chi Chi**. *He picks up his box and exits.*

Methuen Drama Student Editions

Jean Anouilh *Antigone* • John Arden *Serjeant Musgrave's Dance*
Alan Ayckbourn *Confusions* • Aphra Behn *The Rover* • Edward Bond
Lear • *Saved* • Bertolt Brecht *The Caucasian Chalk Circle* • *Fear and
Misery in the Third Reich* • *The Good Person of Szechwan* • *Life of Galileo* •
Mother Courage and her Children • *The Resistible Rise of Arturo Ui* • *The
Threepenny Opera* • Anton Chekhov *The Cherry Orchard* • *The Seagull* •
Three Sisters • *Uncle Vanya* • Caryl Churchill *Serious Money* • *Top Girls*
• Shelagh Delaney *A Taste of Honey* • Euripides *Elektra* • *Medea* •
Dario Fo *Accidental Death of an Anarchist* • Michael Frayn *Copenhagen*
• John Galsworthy *Strife* • Nikolai Gogol *The Government Inspector* •
Robert Holman *Across Oka* • Henrik Ibsen *A Doll's House* • *Ghosts* •
Hedda Gabler • Charlotte Keatley *My Mother Said I Never Should* •
Bernard Kops *Dreams of Anne Frank* • Federico García Lorca *Blood
Wedding* • *Doña Rosita the Spinster* (bilingual edition) • *The House of
Bernarda Alba* • (bilingual edition) • *Yerma* (bilingual edition) • David
Mamet *Glengarry Glen Ross* • *Oleanna* • Patrick Marber *Closer* • John
Marston *Malcontent* • Martin McDonagh *The Lieutenant of Inishmore* •
Joe Orton *Loot* • Luigi Pirandello *Six Characters in Search of an Author*
• Mark Ravenhill *Shopping and F***ing* • Willy Russell *Blood Brothers*
• *Educating Rita* • Sophocles *Antigone* • *Oedipus the King* • Wole
Soyinka *Death and the King's Horseman* • Shelagh Stephenson *The
Memory of Water* • August Strindberg *Miss Julie* • J. M. Synge *The
Playboy of the Western World* • Theatre Workshop *Oh What a Lovely
War* Timberlake Wertenbaker *Our Country's Good* • Arnold Wesker
The Merchant • Oscar Wilde *The Importance of Being Earnest* •
Tennessee Williams *A Streetcar Named Desire* • *The Glass Menagerie*

Methuen Drama Modern Plays

include work by

Edward Albee
Jean Anouilh
John Arden
Margaretta D'Arcy
Peter Barnes
Sebastian Barry
Brendan Behan
Dermot Bolger
Edward Bond
Bertolt Brecht
Howard Brenton
Anthony Burgess
Simon Burke
Jim Cartwright
Caryl Churchill
Noël Coward
Lucinda Coxon
Sarah Daniels
Nick Darke
Nick Dear
Shelagh Delaney
David Edgar
David Eldridge
Dario Fo
Michael Frayn
John Godber
Paul Godfrey
David Greig
John Guare
Peter Handke
David Harrower
Jonathan Harvey
Iain Heggie
Declan Hughes
Terry Johnson
Sarah Kane
Charlotte Keatley
Barrie Keeffe
Howard Korder

Robert Lepage
Doug Lucie
Martin McDonagh
John McGrath
Terrence McNally
David Mamet
Patrick Marber
Arthur Miller
Mtwa, Ngema & Simon
Tom Murphy
Phyllis Nagy
Peter Nichols
Sean O'Brien
Joseph O'Connor
Joe Orton
Louise Page
Joe Penhall
Luigi Pirandello
Stephen Poliakoff
Franca Rame
Mark Ravenhill
Philip Ridley
Reginald Rose
Willy Russell
Jean-Paul Sartre
Sam Shepard
Wole Soyinka
Simon Stephens
Shelagh Stephenson
Peter Straughan
C. P. Taylor
Theatre de Complicite
Theatre Workshop
Sue Townsend
Judy Upton
Timberlake Wertenbaker
Roy Williams
Snoo Wilson
Victoria Wood

Methuen Drama Contemporary Dramatists

include

John Arden (two volumes)
Arden & D'Arcy
Peter Barnes (three volumes)
Sebastian Barry
Dermot Bolger
Edward Bond (eight volumes)
Howard Brenton
  (two volumes)
Richard Cameron
Jim Cartwright
Caryl Churchill (two volumes)
Sarah Daniels (two volumes)
Nick Darke
David Edgar (three volumes)
David Eldridge
Ben Elton
Dario Fo (two volumes)
Michael Frayn (three volumes)
David Greig
John Godber (four volumes)
Paul Godfrey
John Guare
Lee Hall (two volumes)
Peter Handke
Jonathan Harvey
  (two volumes)
Declan Hughes
Terry Johnson (three volumes)
Sarah Kane
Barrie Keeffe
Bernard-Marie Koltès
  (two volumes)
Franz Xaver Kroetz
David Lan
Bryony Lavery
Deborah Levy
Doug Lucie

David Mamet (four volumes)
Martin McDonagh
Duncan McLean
Anthony Minghella
  (two volumes)
Tom Murphy (six volumes)
Phyllis Nagy
Anthony Neilsen (two volumes)
Philip Osment
Gary Owen
Louise Page
Stewart Parker (two volumes)
Joe Penhall (two volumes)
Stephen Poliakoff
  (three volumes)
David Rabe (two volumes)
Mark Ravenhill (two volumes)
Christina Reid
Philip Ridley
Willy Russell
Eric-Emmanuel Schmitt
Ntozake Shange
Sam Shepard (two volumes)
Wole Soyinka (two volumes)
Simon Stephens (two volumes)
Shelagh Stephenson
David Storey (three volumes)
Sue Townsend
Judy Upton
Michel Vinaver
  (two volumes)
Arnold Wesker (two volumes)
Michael Wilcox
Roy Williams (three volumes)
Snoo Wilson (two volumes)
David Wood (two volumes)
Victoria Wood